CITY SLICKERS

MAKE A MILLION IN TWELVE MONTHS

JAMES HIPWELL & ANIL BHOYRUL

CITY SLICKERS

MAKE A MILLION IN TWELVE MONTHS

JAMES HIPWELL & ANIL BHOYRUL

JOHN BLAKE

Published by John Blake Publishing Ltd,
3 Bramber Court, 2 Bramber Road,
London W14 9PB, England

First published in paperback 2000

ISBN 1 90340 200 X

British Library Cataloguing-in-Publication Data:

A catalogue record for this book is
available from the British Library.

Typeset by t2

Printed in Great Britain by
Bookmarque Ltd
Croydon, Surrey

3 5 7 9 10 8 6 4

CONTENTS

Dedicated to the Cairns family

ACKNOWLEDGEMENTS

Just over two years ago, Chancellor Gordon Brown told us he hoped our unconventional style of City journalism would encourage the ordinary man on the street to get a slice of the action in the City. It's taken a long time to turn the Chancellor's vision into reality. First and foremost, we'd like to thank John Blake for giving us the opportunity to do just that by publishing this book — and also for showing faith in us during our darkest hours.

Much of this book has been based on our personal experiences, so we should thank each other. But writing this wouldn't have been possible without the support of the following people in the past few months, especially Mohammed Al Fayed, James Steen, David Price, Sir Richard Branson, Michael Dell (for the freebie computer), Charlie Whelan, Peter Stringfellow, Moya Forsythe, Max Clifford, Matthew Wright, Kevin O'Sullivan, Matt Edwards, Trudi Roche, Ian Ascott, Joan McCarthy, Daisy Bodley, Louise Newman, Jennifer Rontganger, Graham Ellis, John Fashanu, President Omar Bongo (of Gabon), Tom Rubython, Tim Turner, Kath Turner, Sean Nolan, Will Holt, Chris Fowler, Rob Lewis, Tom Bureau, Jonathan Maitland, David Bick, Simon

Cawkwell, Andrew Regan, Tim Blackstone and Jim Mellon.

And a huge thanks to our Mums and Dads, as well as everyone in The Steeles pub in Belsize Park.

CHAPTER ONE

WHO ARE WE?

Okay, let's come clean straight away. We nicked the name City Slickers from the Billy Crystal movie. Over the past few years, the British public has been led to believe that City Slickers — that's us — is meant to be some kind of catchy, punchy description of a couple of guys who know their way round the City. Guys who know where the best deals are, who the biggest players are, and where the hottest action is. Guys with masters degrees in macroeconomics.

Nope. On April 6, 1998, the day before we joined the *Mirror* newspaper to launch a new financial column, our old boss Piers Morgan asked us to come up with a name for it. We happened to be watching the Billy Crystal movie and thought, 'Bingo'.

But don't let that worry you. Our lack of technical knowledge of the financial markets is our main asset. We're just like you, the ordinary punter on the street who wants to make a few bob on shares. That's why the *Mirror* hired us, so ordinary people could understand the City, and get a slice of the action.

A bit of a fluke really, but who cares! Since the two of us first met in 1996 at a party, we discovered straight away we had a lot in common: we both worked in business journalism, but both found it incredibly dull. All that nonsense about profit and loss, price/earnings ratios, analysts' meetings, company results... you name it, we've been bored by it.

But we also had something else in common: common sense. And the truth is, as we've found out hundreds of times, that's all you really need to play the stock market. Sounds too good to be true? Well, the pair of us couldn't always tell a company report from a school report, but we could spot a good share.

And what's a good share? Very simple. One with a

price that shoots up! Never mind whether it's the greatest company in the world, or whether the directors have all just come out of jail for bankruptcy and fraud. We're not interested in the details, or the past, or even the distant future. All we want to know is this: is a company's share price about to shoot up?

So this book is for all you novices, trainees, gamblers, hardened investors — just about anyone who fancies making a bit of cash. It's about how to get a piece of the action in the City.

For too long, the City has been a run by a privileged few, for a privileged few. The pair of us knew that back in 1996 when we first met, and, like most of you, accepted that was the status quo. No-one could ever change it. No-one outside this members-only club could have a say in money matters, let alone benefit from the engine of capitalism.

Over the next few years, as more City doors were shut in our faces, we figured, 'No. This is not right. We want a say.' Initially, through the various newspapers and magazines we worked for together, we played by the rules: never have an opinion; never question the experts; never rock the boat; and, preferably, never dare try and enter this exclusive world.

Things changed dramatically when we joined the *Mirror* newspaper to launch the original City Slickers column in 1998. More by accident than design, our unconventional approach to the City hit a chord with millions of *Mirror* readers. Like us, they were fed up with being shut out from the stock-market revolution. Why shouldn't ordinary people do what the experts do, and have a punt on shares? What's wrong with doubling your cash overnight by investing in a company you've never heard of? What's wrong with getting a broker to give you credit so you can buy and sell shares in a short space of time, without ever having to pay for them — but simply collect a fat cheque for the profits?

Eventually, the clamour of private investors demanding a piece of the action forced the City into change. Today, it's perfectly acceptable for the ordinary man on the street — whether he works at Tesco, whether he cleans your car at the traffic lights or whether he is unemployed, to play the shares game.

The trouble is, as we soon found out, the experts have held on to one last card: refusing to publish anything that explains in ordinary language how you play the stock market. There are hundreds of books and guides out there. We don't believe they are in any way poorly prepared. But to the average man on the street in Britain, they may as well be written in Chinese.

The purpose of this book is to give it to you straight. Right from square one, it tells you exactly where the City is, what it does, and then, most importantly, how to make money out of it. We have covered those dull subjects like price/earnings ratios and net asset values, but in a language you can understand.

As the book goes on, we'll be going into more detail for those of you who might want to make a full-time living out of share trading. And we'll round off with a jargon-buster — the Slickers' official guide to financial terminology. But remember this: you don't need any financial expertise at all to join in. We are by no means experts. All we have mastered is common sense, judgement and intuition.

Or methods on choosing shares may raise eyebrows. They are bizarre, sometimes cynical — even offensive. But we have only one goal in mind: to pick shares where the price will shoot up.

The way we work
Anyone who's had the displeasure of working with us in the past few years knows the one thing we can't

stop doing is having a damn good time. We reckon anyone playing the stock market should do the same. You've probably read all those brochures and even books from the so-called experts. The guys who, by their own admission, 'live, eat and breathe' the stock market. Get a life! Why on earth would anyone want to be so boring?

It is a serious business — don't get us wrong. After all, it's your own dosh you're playing with. But you don't have to come across all serious about it. You can have a good time, honestly.

Say for example you stuck a grand into shares in Sir Alan Sugar's Amstrad, and the next day the price doubled. You've made a grand. You now have two options.

Option one: collect your cheque for a grand profit, and start telling everyone how you did it. How you spotted that his latest product would increase revenue — while at the same time Sir Alan was reducing his exposure on non-revenue enhancing aspects of the business. How the gearing was lowered. How proud you are with the result, and how you now feel part of the company yourself having bought the shares.

Option two: collect your cheque for a grand profit, head straight down Hampstead High Street to buy those Reiss trousers you couldn't afford. Then ring all your mates up for an almighty session in the local boozer, made all the better by the fact you support Arsenal but still made some cash thanks to the Spurs boss.

If you picked option one, you're probably not going to enjoy this book. We recommend you enrol for a degree in Gilts and Bonds at the London School of Economics.

If you picked option two, welcome to the party.

Our track record

You're probably wondering by now why the hell you should believe a word we say. Well, as you've already helped fill our coffers with the £5.99 you paid for this book, it's too late! But, oh yes, we do have an impressive track record, even if we say so ourselves. In January 1999, we produced the 'Top Ten Stocks' for the *Mirror*, for the year ahead. Over the course of the next twelve months, our shares rocketed by an average of 159% — whipping every other newspaper tipster along the way. The incredible thing is, we did the least research but — as we'll keep reminding you over the course of this book — we had the most common sense. Even if we were both nursing huge New Year's Eve party hangovers at the time the tips were written.

Here's just one example — a company called Pace Micro Technology. This is a company that makes set top boxes for satellite television. You know, that odd thing that looks like a CD player that you stick on top of your telly so you can watch Sky Sports.

At the time, in January 1999, digital television had just been launched. Everyone was talking about Rupert Murdoch's BSkyB, and what was likely to happen to the share price as a result.

If you picked up a newspaper that week, you would have been bored to tears by the most complex and comprehensive financial analysis ever given about BSkyB shares. All the papers and all the experts wanted to have their say. The big, burning question was: should you or shouldn't you buy BSkyB shares? The really clever (and really boring) people even managed to do five-year projections on how many satellite dishes BSkyB would sell — and translate that into what the share price would be in five years' time. Great stuff.

But of course, everyone seemed to have missed the point here: you couldn't buy a satellite dish without getting a set top box. Which meant that the one company guaranteed to benefit from all this was Pace Micro Technology. Its shares were just 80p a go at the time. And no one had realised this. We didn't bother researching the company's financials, or the track record of its directors. It was really very simple: this company was about to make heaps of cash, and anyone who bought the shares would do the same. So we advised *Mirror* readers to pile in. They did — and over the next 12 months, the shares went to 800p. That's a gain of 900% in just one year. Try getting that in a building society, or for that matter, on BSkyB shares.

There are countless other examples, which we'll be giving through the course of this book. Sometimes we've spotted a share that we think is worth buying, and literally within days it has shot up by 500%. We have, admittedly, had our fair share of failures. When we started writing this book, our original plan was not to admit to any. But we figured some librarian in the Press Association would read it, and expose us as fraudsters, so we decided to come clean.

Our biggest disaster was a company called Electronics Boutique. This is a company that sells computer games for Playstation and all those other fancy machines. In late 1999, we realised that Playstation 2 was being launched in the Far East — and in the UK in late 2000. Loads of new computer games were being launched to celebrate this event. The biggest winner in all this was surely going to be Electronics Boutique. So we advised *Mirror* readers to stick their cash into the company a.s.a.p. The very next day, the company announced it was in financial trouble (for different reasons) and the shares crashed by 70%.

Oops. Now, you could argue that had we done our research properly, we would have known that. Maybe so — but our game is based on intuition. It can and has gone wrong, but very rarely. We still believe the more loosely you play the market, going on gut feeling, the more success you'll have. In fact, the very next day after the Electronics Boutique shambles, we spotted a little-known company called Pacific Media that said it was about to go big on the Internet. Whenever companies say that, the share price always goes up. But this one hadn't. It was a 'forgotten' company for absolutely no reason, and the share price just 2p. So we told everyone to get stuck in. A week later, the experts in the City also discovered the company — and the price went up by 645%.

The trick is to spot the obvious. That's what we've always done. We've done it in share picking and if you look at other fields, the same always applies. Take Sir Richard Branson. Our favourite Branson story goes back to the Eighties when he launched Virgin Atlantic's first flight to Los Angeles and, as always, took a group of freeloading journalists on the plane to help him celebrate the occasion.

After a few days of all-expenses-paid boozing, Branson and co were checking out of their Hollywood hotel before heading for the airport. One *Sunday Mirror* journalist, rather tired and emotional, staggered up to him and said: 'Richard, I want to be rich and successful like you. But I need an idea that will make me money. Give me a spare idea, 'cos you have loads.' Branson twitched his beard and looked around the hotel foyer, before pointing to an outdoor lamp/heater by the hotel pool (the type you always see outside PizzaExpress).

'I've never seen one of those before. But they are going to be big. Find out who owns them, and buy the UK franchise for them. You'll make a killing.' The franchise was available for £2,000, but the girl in question didn't bother buying it. Ten years later, that franchise is worth £15 million.

Again, just like shares, it's the obvious that you should look for. The stuff that's staring you in the face. That stuff that sounds too good to be true — well usually, it is true.

So how much money can you really make on shares?

The big question is, can you really become a millionaire by dealing in shares? Well, obviously you can. In the same way you could make a million by investing in property, investing in cars, or for that matter sticking all your cash on the 3.30 at Kempton.

There are many ways to make a fortune. However, we strongly believe that dealing in shares can be the most fruitful. Let's not kid ourselves, though: dealing in shares is gambling, pure and simple. There are a few big differences, however, to betting on the horses: Firstly, with a little bit of knowledge, you can greatly increase the chances of winning. Secondly, the amount you win is not fixed — it could be small, reasonable or absolutely huge, and can keep on rising.

But most important is the third difference: unlike any other gamble, how much you lose is entirely up to you. You decide when to cut your losses. Also, you don't have to hand in your chips and pay up if things are going wrong. You have the chance to hang on, hoping for things to turn around. Of course, the amounts you can make depend entirely on what you invest. The more you stick in, the more you can make or lose. Rather than work on amounts, we always think in percentage terms, which gives you a better idea of the possible gains.

When it comes to picking good shares, our idea is to make between 10% and 50% on a good tip — and to make that in a matter of days or, at the most, weeks. More often than not, we're not looking beyond a few days. Over the course of several months on a good share, our idea of a decent return is well over 100%.

That may sound outrageous, but to us that's what share dealing should be about. By deciding to invest in the stock market, you have presumably decided the returns on a building society account are not sufficient. So to us, there is no point thinking you could make 7% that way, whereas this share will only make 6% — so go for the building society. Oh no. Forget 7%. Sure, you might get less on shares, or lose quite a bit. But the gains, when they come, are always worth waiting for.

We mentioned earlier our track record over a year of a 159% return on investment. We don't actually consider that stunning. If you pick ten decent shares to invest in over the course of 12 months, that should be achievable by following our methods, even allowing for a couple of dogs in the portfolio. But during that year, the key is picking some spectacular shares. The ones that rise 500% in the space of a week. We can't guarantee that will happen to you. But we do guarantee this: if you follow our way of playing the stock market, you've got just as good a chance — if not better — of cashing in on the City than the experts.

So let's play!

CHAPTER TWO
FOOL'S GUIDE TO CAPITALISM

Where is the City?

That's a good question, especially if you don't live in London. The word 'City' is actually misleading. We've always thought, and still do, that the City is just a place where lots of people live and work. So if you work in Salford, you work in the City. Except if you say that everyone will fall about laughing. In fact, the City's definition of itself is so biased that people who work there like to distinguish themselves from those in London's West End, even though it's only a couple of miles away.

Traditionally, the City has been confined to the Square Mile. If you got a tube map out, that's somewhere between Moorgate and Bank on the Northern Line, going across to Liverpool Street on the Central Line.

The centre of it is the Bank of England on Threadneedle Street. For some bizarre reason, the bank is referred to as the 'Old Lady of Threadneedle Street'. We've no idea why, and don't see much point in finding out. After all, apart from the Bank's Governor, Eddie George, and his staff, there's no reason why you would possibly want to go there. For starters, there's not even a Link machine in sight, which is odd given that this is meant to be the mother of all banks.

Over many years, all the big banks and financial companies have tried to base themselves as near to the Big Bank as possible. Most are just round the corner in Bishopsgate, and just about every stockbroking firm is scattered around there. In our opinion, it's the second worst place to work in Britain, next to Canary Wharf. Which is why many big banks are now moving to, yes, you guessed it, Canary Wharf. Both places, especially the first one, are completely dead by 7pm. Most of these guys finish work at 4.30pm, get absolutely hammered and are in bed by 6pm.

Our advice is, never ever go there. You should never have to anyway. The people are mostly stuck up their own egos, there are very few single women and everyone buys bottles of expensive champagne that they don't drink. No way, José.

What's the point of it?

Very simply, to make wads of dosh. Whether we like it or not, our lives are ruled by capitalism. In other words, every single thing we do is governed by the chance to make a few quid.

Governments, dictatorships, royal families and the rest of them are all well and good, especially for tourism. But the real power is in the City. It's a bit like one gigantic football stadium, where every team plays each other every day. But unlike the FA Cup, if you lose you get another chance the next day. And the best thing about it is that the supporters — people like you and us — can get a game as well.

The idea of the City — or rather the stock market — is for companies from all over the world to test themselves out against each other. Like one big casino. Public companies all have products and services, and they use the City to raise money (mostly from people like you and me) to make more products and sell more products. Loads of other people, such as analysts and stockbrokers, spend their time like referees, deciding who's having a better game at any moment in time. The ones who do well see their shares prices go up, and the ones doing badly get a pasting. We 'fans' can have a punt on the best teams, and if we call it right, we're quids in too. This might sound too simplistic, but that's really all there is to it. The thing is, imagine how much money we're talking about here: literally trillions and trillions of pounds (or euros, if you're that way inclined).

Such capitalist ideas have been around for donkey's years. Between the sixteenth and eighteenth century, many shipping companies were formed that borrowed money from rich people. They'd sail off round the world, discover gold and hopefully come back with masses of cash, given back to their original 'shareholders'. The first ever such company to be formed was called 'The Mysterie and Companie of the Merchant Adventurers for the Discoverie of Regions, Dominions, Islands and Places Unknown (1553)'.

Sounds to us like a typical twenty-first-century dot.com stock.

By the 1690s, with share trading growing, many specialist brokers would meet in the Royal Exchange to carry out their deals. They were a pretty loud bunch and most eventually got banned from the building. The fashion then became to congregate around the many coffee shops in Threadneedle Street, where most of the share trading was done. Two shops, Jonathan's and Garraway's, were the centre of most of the activity. In 1762, a group of brokers tried to get exclusive use of Jonathan's coffee shop but failed. So they raised the cash between them to buy their own coffee shop, 'New Jonathan's' which, in 1773, became the world's first-ever stock exchange. However, the premises weren't perfect, so in 1801 the members raised £20,000 to take over derelict premises in Capel Court. This has remained the site of the exchange ever since.

In 1802, the stock exchange became a formal body (although most of the guys who work there still do a lot of business in the coffee shops) with 550 subscribers and 100 clerks. Other regional exchanges were opened around the UK and all were amalgamated into the London Stock Exchange in 1973.

How does it work?

The mainstay of the City is the stock market — those thousands of companies you see listed in the *Financial Times* every morning. Companies in Britain have two choices — being either privately owned, or publicly owned. The public ones are all part of the stock market. There are two easy ways to spot a public company. First, it has plc stuck on the end of its name (public limited company). Second, there are usually a number of ex-Tory ministers or members of the House of Lords who appear as non-executive directors. These people generally get paid 15 grand a year to let a company use their name, to help attract investors. Nice work if you can get it.

In almost all cases, the reason for going public (and therefore joining the stock market and becoming part of the City) is for expansion. Mr Smith, who sells potatoes for a living in South Charlton, realises one day that he is probably the best potato seller in Britain. Except to do that, his company Smith Potatoes would need about five million quid — to pay for extra lorries, potatoes, etc. So he applies to join the stock market. Smith Potatoes Ltd, previously 100% owned by him, now becomes Smith Potatoes plc. Now it's 40% owned by him, and 60% owned by outside investors. (This ratio varies in every public company).

These are usually a few big City institutions who like lending money (fund managers and banks), and the rest are people like me and you who decide to buy shares in Smith Potatoes plc. Mr Smith no longer owns all of the company, but he now has the five million quid he needed. So, on day one of being public, anyone can buy shares in Smith Potatoes plc. The institutions initially set the share price — for example, they break it down into 50 million shares all worth 10p each. As time goes by, if the company does well the price goes up and vice versa if it fails. The big advantage for a company going public is that it has a lot more cash than before and, if things go really well, the people who started it all off can make a fortune because they've got loads of the shares.

The biggest advantage of going public is obviously to raise loads of cash. But it does have disadvantages. For starters, your company's value is subject to outside influence. If the stock market crashes, you're going to lose loads of money.

Companies in the stock market are also subject to masses of scrutiny. Every single move they make is analysed and often made public. That's why many old-fashioned banks have stayed private. Even Richard Branson's Virgin Group is private. The tycoon did float his company in the Eighties, but got fed up of having to answer to the City — so he bought it back off the shareholders again a few years later.

There is, of course, a lot more to the City than the stock market. Currency trading, bonds, gilts — all sorts of other things you could get excited about. But you have to be a bit of an expert to get involved in that. If that's what excites you, we suggest you buy another book. As far as we're concerned, the only thing that real matters for private investors is the stock market.

The main players in the City

Stockbrokers

Our usual image of the City is loads of blokes in pin-striped suits sitting in front of computer screens, on the phone, waving their hands frantically. Don't be fooled by this: most of these guys are actually placing bets on the football and have nothing to do with the workings of the City. The cameras rarely film City people at work.

Any financial market contains a host of characters, the most important being the stockbrokers, analysts, fund managers and market makers — although not in that order. As far as we're concerned, the people you need to worry most about are the stockbrokers. These are the guys dealing in your hard-earned cash — and they often make serious mistakes.

Brokers are the link between us private investors and the big money. We think of them as telephone receptionists — that's pretty much what they are. You ring them up and say you want to buy some shares, and they ring their mates in the City and buy them for you. And that's about it! In fact, these days they don't even do that very much — usually they just press a button on a computer. Oh, and they do send you a bill for their services (normally about 1.5% of the amount of cash you spend).

There's absolutely no reason for any stockbroker to be anywhere near the City, although many are for historical or pose reasons. That said, the best ones are to be found outside London. As we'll explain later, our advice is to find some small-time broker out in the country that no-one's ever heard of. He'll charge you less and, more importantly, he's always there when you want him — unlike most big-name brokers.

Until a few years ago (before the introduction of electronic trading), all brokers dealt with jobbers. These chaps worked on the floor of the Stock Exchange, and held a number of shares for buying and selling. After you rang up a broker, he rang up his mate on the dealing floor with your order — his mate then tried to buy or sell the shares on your behalf from the jobber. The jobber always quoted two prices — the ask price (selling price) and the bid price (buying price). The difference between the two is where everyone made their commission. A pretty simple system, although it got pretty chaotic. Thanks to technological advances and increased competition, it was all change. The market could no longer support both specialised jobbing firms and brokers acting as middlemen. The only solution was to abandon this division.

As more money was needed, the big players all seized their chance to get a slice of the action. In the Eighties, foreign banks and dealing houses, high-street banks and merchant banks between them swallowed the largest jobbing and broking firms — creating the large financial conglomerates that now carry out much of the business in the City. The smaller broking firms still remain, but most trading is now done electronically.

Until late 1997, the backbone of the London Stock Exchange trading system was SEAQ (Stock Exchange Automated Quotations). This carried the prices of over 2,000 securities (a posh word for stocks) direct to the offices of brokers. This was pretty straightforward stuff, based on a so-called 'quote-driven system'. (If this is getting too technical, don't worry. A bit of history is always handy, though.) What it meant was the computer screens showed the bid and offer (buy and sell) prices on a stock. The best of each were automatically highlighted and your broker could press a button and get or sell the shares you wanted.

This all changed again in 1997, with the introduction of SETS (Stock Exchange Electronic

Trading Service). The subtle but huge difference is that this is now order driven rather than quote driven. This matches buyers and sellers instantly, and different prices can be obtained by your broker. In other words, if he wants, the broker can get you a much better deal than before, with a variety of payment options.

Most trading is now done this way, although for some smaller shares where there isn't a huge market, more traditional methods are still used.

Analysts

Away from all this mayhem probably the most important group of City people are the analysts. You're never likely to meet one of these guys, which is just as well as you'd probably want to punch them in the face. They are the crowd who basically, as the name suggests, analyse everything. Whatever they say goes. If, for example, the analysts decide they don't really like Marks & Spencer (as they all did in 1999), you can be pretty sure the share price comes crashing down.

The City hangs on their every word, as they are the 'experts' passing judgement on a company's fate. Whenever a public company has anything to announce, its directors usually announce it to the analysts first, before the journalists. The analysts then make public their feelings, and those of us with shares in that company prey to God that they like what they hear.

All year round, analysts put out their views — on how much money a company will make, what it's doing right or wrong. Getting analysts on side is the most important task of a company chairman. Even Rupert Murdoch is known to spend time wooing top analysts over lunch to get them on side.

Institutional investors

You are bound to keep hearing about these guys: they are the real money men. These are the lot who hold billions of pounds in cash (coming from pension funds and other sources) which they then invest in companies. The institutions usually have large stakes in most of Britain's biggest companies. If you look down the share registers of any, you will find at least 20% owned by at least one big institution.

Private investors like us have nothing at all to do with these guys. However, their decisions have a huge impact on us. If you had shares in, for example Psion, and one of the big institutions decided to sell its 20% holding in the company, the price would plummet. And there is nothing you could do about it.

Because of this, as you'll notice, we generally stay away from investing in big companies. Our tactics are all about being ahead of the game. When a big institution has hundreds of millions of pounds invested in a company, it's very unlikely you can beat them at their own game. After all, if they had reason to believe the shares were about to rise (and they would know before you), they would buy loads before you could.

Types of market

The one we always hear about is the Footsie. This is the trendy word of the FTSE-100 — the index of the 100 biggest companies (by size) in the UK. It was created in 1983, and its performance every day generally reflects what's happening in the City. If you hear the FTSE-100 is down massively, that pretty much means most other shares are down. It's the Premier League of shares, containing mega-companies such as British Telecom and BP Amoco. Loads of companies would give anything to be in this prestigious list, as many institutions invest in all the companies all the time. If you're in, you're onto a winner.

That said, because the companies are so big, it's the last place for private investors like us to look for a quick profit. If British Telecom announces some new mega-deal, the shares would rise no more than 5–6%. That would be seen as a huge leap and a massive surge. But if you held £1,000 of shares in BT, that would just about be enough to buy you a decent meal.

There are exceptions, which we'll come on to later, but for the most part, companies in the FTSE-100 are not going to drastically improve your finances, unless you're prepared to hold on to them for at least 10 years. They are more the 'building society' option — a reasonably safe bet over a period of a couple of years.

Outside the FTSE-100 are thousands of other companies — some appear in different indices such as Techmark (a listing of technology stocks). Basically, the further down the list you go, the more likely you are to make a fast buck — or lose an absolute fortune.

Not all companies immediately join the full stock exchange. In recent years, there has been a massive surge of interest in AIM — the Alternative Investment Market. To get into the main market, you need to demonstrate an impressive track record, with years of well-kept accounts behind you. For many small companies, this is out the question. AIM is their answer, as the rules for getting in are less stringent. It's where you'll find plenty of small start-up Internet companies, and where, in our opinion, the real money is to be made.

Outside the stock exchange is the Ofex market — this is for unregulated companies. Or, to put it another way, companies that have virtually no history — but plenty of hope. You find a lot of companies with bizarre ideas on there — like how to turn water into gold. Entry to Ofex is decided by a panel of 'wise men' from the broker JP Jenkins. The only requirement is that companies must publish their accounts twice a year. Put it this way — if this book sells well, we'll probably form City Slickers Ltd and try and get on Ofex to make ourselves rich! This is clearly the riskiest place to buy shares, though as we'll explain later, there are a few punts worth having.

For the most part, our advice is stick to small companies on the main market or companies on AIM. For what its worth, about 90% of the companies we've ever bought shares in are listed on the AIM market.

Types of shares

If you thought understanding markets was complicated enough, the bad news is that understanding the different types of share is ten times worse. We're going to take you through them in as simple a way as possible — but don't be too alarmed. The thing to remember is that for the most part, when you buy shares, all you'll have to do is ring up a broker and say, 'Get me some of these, mate.' But it's worth knowing the various types.

Ordinary shares

When you make that call, the chances are the broker

will be buying you so-called 'ordinary shares' (in fact, he'll always do that unless you tell him otherwise). Most shares in a company are classified as ordinary shares — they are the price you see listed in the paper and on telly. If you buy them and hang on to them, you get voting rights — so you can turn up at the company's Annual General Meeting and cause mayhem, or even stand for the chairman's job yourself, if you really want to be awkward.

The rewards and risks are the highest — these are the shares where the price goes up and down the most. Every six months, companies pay out a dividend (if they are doing well). It's entirely up to the company how much to pay out, but if you've bought shares on the basis of making a living from the dividend, forget it. On average, if you have a grand's worth of shares in a company, you'll be lucky to get £50 a year in dividends.

The downside of ordinary shares is that if the company happens to go bust, you can forget your investment. Ordinary shareholders are last in line to get any money back — in most cases, they get absolutely nothing.

But we suggest you don't worry about that. Share-dealing is gambling after all, and ordinary shares are your best bet.

Preference shares

The name suggests some sort of preferential treatment, but don't let anyone massage your ego and try to get you to buy some. These are distributed by some major companies, like the Bank of Scotland and Shell. The advantage of them is they generally pay a higher dividend — more like a fixed income. It's pretty similar to putting your money in a building society. But the downside, and it's a huge downside, is that you don't get the chance to make a killing when the share price shoots up — because these are priced differently.

And, to really rub your nose in it, there are no voting rights that go with these, so you can't even turn up at the Annual General Meeting and make a nuisance of yourself.

Share sectors

As we just said, you should only ever need to deal with ordinary shares. The key is to decide which ones. There is no real official breakdown of share sectors, although most companies fall into one or other sector. For example, you wouldn't class BT shares in the same sector as PizzaExpress.

The *Financial Times* and most other papers list shares in different sectors each morning, but these sectors aren't much of a guide to investment. The following is the way we have generally broken down shares.

Blue-chip shares

There isn't a formal definition of 'blue chips' as such, but the term generally refers to large, well-established, well-run companies. The big boys such as Unilever, British Telecom, Vodafone — all the mega-companies, which are mostly in the FTSE-100.

All the big financial institutions usually have a big stake in these companies, because over a period of a few years, they are expected to rise steadily. If, for example, you stuck a grand in Boots, you should get a few hundred quid profit over a few years. There's a good chance of doing better than a building society account, and these are the shares many families and OAPs go for — a kind of safe bet.

And a pretty unexciting bet! Because the financial institutions have big stakes in these companies, they know them inside out. So as a private investor, your chances of spotting something new, hearing something exclusive or just having a hunch are between zero and zero. It's almost unheard of to get a massive pay day from these. Don't get us wrong — some stocks like British Telecom have been known to go up 100% in one year, which isn't bad by any standards. But that is a rarity.

And don't let anyone tell you that blue chips are safe as houses. The original Rolls-Royce went bust in 1971 and, more recently, British & Commonwealth collapsed despite the efforts of its boss, John Gunn. Both disasters cost many shareholders their life savings, in what seemed at the time two of the safest shares you could buy.

Growth stocks

These are the ones we'll be talking about most, as they are the private Investor's dream. They are generally companies in the high-tech and Internet sector, where the price keeps shooting up — regardless of what the rest of the stock market is doing. Sure, there's the odd market correction, but all in all, this is where we reckon the action is.

They are hard to find, but there are plenty of them out there. You can also pick up a few in established sectors such as biotechnology. Every now and again, some company somewhere is about to discover a cancer-busting drug. It never actually does, but as the rumour mill swings into overdrive, you can double your money.

Defensive shares

We're back to the so-called 'grandmother' shares

again. These shares are pretty solid ones, which are unlikely to fall even in a nuclear war. They are to be found in essential service industries — such as food, gas, petrol and those sorts of companies. No matter how bad things are, everyone still pops down to Tesco on a Saturday — but they never buy more than they usually do. In other words, you should be safe with these but not much else.

Recovery stocks

These are another bunch that we're pretty keen on. As the name suggests, they are shares that are currently going through a disastrous patch — but have a good chance of recovering. Getting these at the height of their disaster can be a good thing.

If, for example, British Gas announced tomorrow that it was running out of cash, sacking half the workforce and getting a new management team, the shares would probably dive 40%. Which means you should buy them — gas is an essential commodity, and you know this stock will be back up there pretty soon.

Cyclical stocks

These are a bit too long term for our liking, but there is the chance to make serious dosh out of them. They are the kind of shares whose fortunes vary depending on various outside factors, such as the economy, weather, the World Cup etc. Take restaurants — in a deep recession, we're less likely to go for a slap-up meal and will probably head straight down the boozer instead. So shares in restaurants generally go down in a recession, but can be sure to recover.

Even football is affected — during Euro 96, football memorabilia sales shot up. If you had shares in the company selling England shirts, you would have done well. Until the Germans dumped us out on penalties.

Highly rated stocks

These are similar to growth stocks, but the price is already very high. Generally the company hasn't done anything yet, but investors are confident it's about to do something big. We're not huge fans of these, as the price is too high and expectations even higher.

Small companies and penny shares

Now we're talking! These are the bread and butter of the City Slickers. Small companies, if spotted at the right time, can make you an absolute fortune. We gave you the example earlier on of Pace Micro Technology, and how you could have made over 500% on your money in a year with that company.

There are far better examples (which we missed

out on). Take the little-known computer firm called International Tabulator. That grew to become IBM, one of the world's biggest companies. Ten years ago, Dell Computers was a tin-pot company no-one had heard of. Now it's as big as IBM. Michael Dell himself told us that if we had bunged $10,000 into Dell Computers when it floated, our shareholding today would be worth around $2 million — yes, $2,000,000.

These are by nature the riskiest of investments, as for every success story there are a hundred failures. But they are out there each day, waiting to be invested in. Many small companies are penny shares, though the definition of penny shares is one where the price is under 100p and where the difference between the buying and selling price is more than 10%. That's all a bit too technical for us. Our idea of penny shares is literally that. Take a mining company called Bula Resources, whose shares were 2p. A bit of good news came out and the shares went to 6p. So, after broker commissions, you've more than doubled your money! You won't get that with BT — no matter how upbeat the announcement.

Working out how good a company is

As we said earlier, we don't subscribe to the view that you need to be a financial expert to spot a good share.

Most of our dealings are made on hunches. Sadly though, it's impossible to read a newspaper or journal without some reference to a company's financials. Sometimes — though rarely — the figures can be useful. In our view, there are a handful of financial statistics of a company that are worth knowing. But don't be too worried if you don't fully understand these. Noone ever got rich by being obsessed with stochastics!

Price/earnings ratios

The word everyone keeps going on about in the City is the p/e ratio, or 'earnings multiple' as it is known, of a company. 'Have you see the crazy p/e Amstrad is on? Incredible! Amazing!' is a query you are likely to hear if you frequent bars around Liverpool Street. We recommend you stay away from these places, but there's nothing clever about the p/e ratio. All you need to really know is that the higher it is, the faster the company is growing.

The mathematical way to work out a p/e ratio is to divide the current share price by the earnings per share. This is easier than you think. Take company John Smith plc for example, which has an imaginary share price of 500p. It makes annual profits after tax of £20 million, and there are 50 million shares around. So the earnings per share is 20 million divided by 50 million — which is £0.4, or 40p.

The p/e ratio is therefore 500/40, which is 12.5.

The next question is, how high is this? Well, p/e ratios are primarily used in comparison. If, for example, John Smith manufactured aeroplanes and most rival aeroplane manufacturers had a p/e ratio of 50, then you can safely say John Smith plc is either a disaster or incredibly cheap. Then again, if rival companies had a p/e of 5, things are looking pretty good.

When you look at share prices in newspapers, you often find a column with the p/e ratio alongside the prices. It's really just a case of checking out the number against those of other companies in the same sector.

Later in this book we'll be talking about building a portfolio and how you can make longer-term investments. But for the purpose of making a quick buck, the p/e ratio is a waste of time. It isn't going to affect whether a company's share price doubles overnight — so don't get too despondent if you are scratching your head right now.

Dividend yield

This is the good one to bore your mates with down the pub. Although it's a term used by many investors, we have to admit that it has never been of any use whatsoever when deciding whether or not to buy a share.

Quite simply, 'dividend yield' means the dividend per share (net of tax), divided by the share price. As with the p/e ratio, this is only useful in comparison. You can judge how much money your shares are earning compared to other shares you have, by comparing this figure. Like we said, it's never struck us as a useful tool, even though people keep going on about it.

If you want to get technical, stick with p/e ratios.

Net asset value
Again, a nice phrase but little use when it comes to share picking. The definition of net asset value is the value of a company's net assets (all the things it owns, minus its liabilities) divided by the number of ordinary shares. So in other words, it's a kind of measure of what each share is worth — the concrete value underlying each share.

Market capitalisation
Alongside p/e ratios, this is the main bit of jargon we've found useful over the years. The market capitalisation is, as the name suggests, the value of a company. This, of course, changes every second, depending on the

share price at that moment in time. To work it out, you multiply the number of ordinary shares in the company by the price of the shares.

We've found it very useful to know this figure so we can judge whether a company's share price will rise following some event. As always, how you judge a good or bad market value is up to the individual. Take for example some small Internet company with a market capitalisation of £10 million, which is planning to do a mega-deal with Freeserve that will treble its income. To us, it's obvious the market capitalisation is very low and the deal will see it rise — by a rise in the share price. So we'd get the shares.

More importantly, the figure is useful when deciding not to buy shares. Quite often, companies have a very high market capitalisation, even though they haven't done anything. This is because the City is expecting them to do something good in the future, and the shares have already risen in anticipation. So if you hear about a great new deal, check the market value first. If it seems too high, or has risen ten-fold in the past year, the new deal isn't going to give the shares much of a lift because it is already reflected in the price.

You can find the market capitalisation of every listed company in the *Financial Times* every Monday. Or save yourself the trouble by getting it any time off most financial websites.

Company reports

A lot of people are, for some mysterious reason, fascinated by company reports. They seem to get a kick out of collecting them, like a record collection that they can show off to their friends after a few drinks. And they study them astutely in the morning, familiarising themselves with every detail of the company. There's nothing wrong with that, if that's the sort of person you are. But there's one very important thing to remember about company reports: they are published a long time after the official results, so there are very rarely any bombshells or hidden gems to be found. And if there are, the odds are that thousands of other investors have already discovered them.

Come to think of it, you'll never find some great piece of news hidden away in a company report that is going to make you a fortune. If there is good news, the company will tell the world and his brother first. More than often, it's bad news that is tucked away in reports. Journalists like us scan through them because they publish the salaries of directors, which always makes a good story.

CHAPTER THREE

GETTING STARTED

Getting a computer

People often ask us how much money you need to be able to invest in shares. The truth is you can do it without spending a penny, as we'll be showing you. But some basic and small investments can make a huge difference. The simplest of these, we reckon, is a computer with connection to the Internet. You can grab one from Dixons for less than £600 these days, and it's well worth it. Why? In the past two years the Internet has changed everything, and almost all the information you want on a company can be found through it. There are loads of financial websites that give you a daily update on what's happening in the market — uk-invest.co.uk, TheStreet.co.uk, Bloomberg.com, iii.co.uk to name but a few. Our favourite is FreeQuotes.com. As the name suggest, it gives you instant and immediate share prices. Interactive Investor International (iii.co.uk) is also pretty handy, as it often carries live breaking news.

What people often forget, absurd as it seems, is that share prices change by the second. It's all very well helping yourself to a grand of shares in a company and then ringing your mates up to tell them what you've just done. In the space of 15 minutes, the price may have shot up — and back down again. You would have missed your chance to make a killing because you were too busy boring your mates to tears about the investment. And you can be sure your broker isn't going to phone you and tell you the good news. He's too busy selling the shares for everyone else who has noticed the price has risen.

This doesn't mean you have to spend your life in front of a computer screen watching share prices change, but in many cases if you're hoping for a quick buck, it's up to you to monitor the share prices. And the only proper way to do that is with a computer. You can get most prices on Teletext, but it can take forever and the prices are often at least 15 minutes old.

If you end up getting into share dealing big time, it's worth considering the next option: getting a Reuters terminal. It's what many City experts use, and for private users can be rented out for around £500 a month. This is basically a computer screen with live share prices on display. You can pull up the share price of any company but, unlike the Internet, it gives you far more information, much of which is surprisingly useful. For a start, each time shares are bought in that company, the deal is actually seen going through on the screen. Even if you buy 50 quid's worth, it will register the deal. This is quite handy to find out where the action is. If you spot that 50 million quid's worth of shares have been bought in the last hour in a small company, and the price is rising, you can be pretty sure some action is about to happen — and get some shares yourself.

About a year ago, we noticed this happening at a company called Lionheart on our Reuters screen. To be honest, we had no idea what the company did, but spotted that loads of shares had been bought in the previous half an hour. And the price had gone from 12p to 16p as a result. So we got on the phone to our broker and booked £1,250 worth of shares each, at 17p a go. The price kept going up, to 20p — then, about half an hour later, the company announced some big Internet deal. The price rocketed to 43p instantly, and we sold out. We'd made nearly £2,000 each in less than an hour, on a company we didn't even know existed!

Reuters is also very good for historical information, so you can instantly find out everything that's ever been said about a company. If someone down a pub tells you that Marks & Spencer is about to be sold for £4 billion, you'd probably think 'Great!' and buy as many shares as possible. Then again, if you checked on the Reuters screen you'd realise that the rumour has been going around for a year and nothing's happened yet. This is especially handy for smaller companies, whose news and rumours aren't that widely reported by the national press.

If you do decide to get a Reuters terminal, you'll probably keep hearing about the rival Bloomberg terminal. That's pretty good too, but it's more expensive. And for private investors, our opinion is that it's too complicated. It also involves getting a huge brown lead drilled through your living room, which is enough to put anyone off. Don't get us wrong — in many ways, Bloomberg is actually better than Reuters, and the company's founder, Mike

Bloomberg, is an old mate of ours, so we don't want to annoy him. But Bloomberg is better for the experts, which we are not.

Brokers or banks?

There are various ways to buy shares, the most common being through a broker, bank or on the Internet. Trading on line is a growing industry and has a lot of advantages — we'll be talking about that more later on. However, for the private and first-time investor, the choices are really a bank or a broker.

There's no choice, as far as we're concerned: you have to get a broker. The reason is that if you buy shares through a bank (which in turn does the deal through a broker), you have one massive disadvantage: you can't sell them again until you receive the share certificate, which can take up to six weeks if not longer. This is a huge problem, which many people overlook to their disadvantage.

Say you buy shares in British Airways because you hear about some great new, profitable route they are about to launch. The shares are 300p each. You get a grand's worth through your bank, and bingo — a week later the deal is announced. The shares rise to 370p on the news. You're over the moon. You've made over £200 profit in a week.

Unfortunately, you can't sell the shares because you are waiting for the share certificate. By the time it comes through, thousands of other shareholders have sold out at 370p, and the price collapses to 290p. You're now £50 down on the deal — even though you were smart enough to get the shares before it was announced.

Buying shares through a bank can be even more disastrous than that. When you decide to sell them, you usually have about two weeks to produce the share certificate (as proof you own the shares). Even though we say it takes up to six weeks to get them, there is no way of knowing exactly how long you have to wait. Sometimes, soon after buying shares through a bank, investors get overexcited when they see the price shoot up, so they ring the bank and sell the shares after a couple of weeks, confident the certificate will be with them soon.

It doesn't appear, and you are then forced into a 'buy back' — which means you then have to buy back the shares that you sold, because technically speaking you never owned them in the first place. By now, the price may have risen even further. It's not uncommon for people to lose £1,000 this way, when they should really have been making that amount on their shares. So in other words, stay well away from a bank when it comes to share dealing.

Which takes us to getting a stockbroker. The first question is, which one? If you get the Yellow Pages, you'll find some listed there (most don't advertise, as it's not considered the right thing to do in the City, for some strange reason). The chances are you will have heard of the big names. The temptation is to get registered with one of these, because they are seen as 'reliable'.

They are, but our advice is stay away from them. The problem with the big names, especially since the middle of 1999, is that everyone wants to use them. Such has been the growth in share dealing, these guys are up to their necks in business — so your investment is not going to make a big difference to them. The first problem you'll have with a big-name stockbroker is getting through. We know loads of people who have waited for over half an hour on the phone, in the queue to speak to their stockbroker. That's bad news if you're desperately trying to buy a share that is moving up by the second. It's disastrous news if you're trying to sell as the price collapses. Hanging on the telephone for ten minutes could cost you 20% of your investment.

Our worst own case was a restaurant company

called BGR, which we stuck £1,000 into in 1999, purely on a rumour that good things were going to happen. The rumour turned out to be false and the price suddenly slipped 3%. We thought, 'Never mind, win some, lose some' and decided to sell. Our broker was engaged at the time — so we wondered over to the coffee machine before trying again. By the time we got back with our cappuccinos, the price was 5% down — everyone was selling. We got through to the broker and cut our losses at £200. Imagine if you had to wait half an hour — by then the price was 14% down, as everyone was panic selling.

As most stockbrokers are concentrated in London, our advice is to find one outside the capital — preferably as far away as possible. Brokers are brokers — don't let anyone tell you otherwise. They will buy you the same shares at the same price. But if you're registered with a smaller broker, you have a much better chance of getting through when you want to, and the broker is more likely to take an interest in your affairs because your business matters to him.

Technically speaking, there are various types of services brokers can offer. The cheapest is known as 'execution-only', whereby the broker does what you tell him and nothing else. You could choose other services such as 'Execution and Advice', whereby he gives you his opinion for a fee. Or for long-term investments, some kind of portfolio management. Our experience is that once you get to know a broker, he'll start giving you advice anyway. So you might as well opt for the cheaper execution-only service.

The costs vary between brokers. Most charge anything between 1.25–1.75% commission on any deals, so if you buy £1,000 worth of shares in any company, you'll have to pay him between £12.50 and £17.50 for his efforts. It really isn't worth shopping around for the cheapest broker — just go for the one that seems low key and happy to deal with you. You can also get a list of brokers from the Association of Private Client Investment Managers and Stockbrokers (APCIMS). They can be contacted on 020 7247 7080.

Types of account

Assuming you've found a broker, the next decision is which type of account to go for. There are two main choices — in your own name, or in a nominee account.

For private investors, you might as well register in your own name. Every time you buy and sell a share, the broker sends you a contract note telling you what you've done, how much you owe or how much you've made. Using a broker, you can sell the shares even if you don't have the certificate — you just need to keep the contract note as proof you bought them.

As you get more experienced, you might want to open a nominee account. This is a way in which the broker holds all the paperwork on your behalf. He sets up a nominee account for you. One advantage of doing this is that your name never appears on share registers, or anywhere else. So nobody knows who actually bought and sold specific shares (not even the company you bought them in). If, for some reason, you don't want anyone to know what you are up to, then go for a nominee account.

Paying for shares

This is the key to getting started in share dealing: don't pay! That may sound ridiculous, but it really is easy to do when you first start out.

If you buy shares the traditional way, through a bank, obviously you have to pay for them in the normal way. But as we said earlier, we suggest you stay well away from banks. Later, we'll be talking about building a portfolio, where again you need some ready cash to make some serious long-term cash.

But initially, it is possible to get away with it by using a 'T+' system. This is how it works: brokers give clients a specific number of days to settle the account — generally five, ten, or fifteen (he'll tell you the options you have on specific shares). So, for example, you decide to buy £5,000 worth of shares in Internet company Lastminute.com. You ring up the broker, and he says you can have it on a T+10 basis. This means you have ten working days after buying the shares to settle the trade. The important thing to remember here is that settling the account doesn't necessarily mean paying up for the shares. In practice, it means you have ten working days to either pay for them, or sell them.

If, before the ten days are up, you sell them, your trade is now settled. Should the share price have gone up within those ten days, you get a cheque from the broker for the profit you've made (minus his commission). On the other hand, if the price has dropped and you sell them, you then have to pay him for the difference.

Once you've registered with a broker, you should get a credit limit on your account — normally between £2,000 and £10,000. Which means you have quite a lot of cash to play with.

The next thing to remember when paying for shares is that, unlike the prices you see in the FT, the broker will always give you two prices: the bid and ask price (the selling and buying price). The selling price is always lower than the buying price. The difference, known as the spread, is where the brokers and market makers make the rest of their commission.

So let's see how this would work with that example of buying shares in Lastminute.com: You ring up the broker and say you want £5,000 worth of shares. The bid price is 200p and the ask price is 208p. He buys you around 2,400 shares in the company on a T+10 basis.

You now have ten working days to decide what to do next. Presumably, you haven't actually got the five grand handy to pay up — we never do! But you're hoping the price will rise within ten days. The crucial thing to remember here is that the SELLING price has to rise above 208p for you to make any cash. If, say, the price goes up 5p during the ten days, you would have thought you'd be in profit. Unfortunately not — the selling price would be around 205p, which means that you would still lose out even though the price has risen.

If, during that period the selling price rises to 240p and you sell, you should now be sitting on shares worth £5,760 — a profit of £760. After taking his commission, the broker will then send you a cheque for around £700. Simple as that! So without ever having had the five grand, you've bagged a £700 profit.

Of course, this can work the other way if the price drops and you might end up owing the broker that amount, but that's the gamble you take. If you do it sensibly, it's a reasonably safe gamble. Barring a stock market crash, it's unlikely most shares will fall more than 20% in ten days. The way to guard against this is to work out how much you can afford to lose: say it's £200. In that case, only buy £1,000 worth of shares, so if things do go wrong and the price falls 20%, you will only lose £200.

The T+ system is very common, and once you get up and running, you can end up having a punt every few days, as long as you've settled your account. In theory, you could have a £5,000 punt each morning on a share you think will rise 10%. If you get just one right a week, you'll make £2,000 a month. The trouble is, you'll also have to pay the difference for the ones where the price fell.

Getting set for your first share deal
It's now getting close to the big day — when you actually buy your first share. There are many schools

of thought on how and when to do this — most so-called experts believe you should do months of research, save up a lot of cash and have your house kitted out with £10,000 worth of technology before you kick off. We don't. In our experience, it's best to have a small punt first, just to get a feel for the market. Don't expect to make a fortune, but be sensible so that you don't lose one.

We reckon that after about two to three weeks of reading the business pages, watching the business news on telly and so on, you should have a basic idea of what's happening in the City. Don't be alarmed by this — we just mean knowing basic things. If, for example, the news for the past week has been that the stock market is crashing or is about to crash, it may not be a good time to invest.

If every morning you read about how, for example, PizzaExpress is in last-ditch talks with its bankers to avoid going bust, it's not a good idea to buy the shares. That may sound obvious but it still amazes us how many people get it badly wrong on their first investment. People's first share they buy usually has some sort of emotional value — they go for shares in Charlton Athletic because it's their favourite football team, even if the side is two games away from relegation. Or they go for shares in British

Airways for some patriotic reason, even if the airline is about to announce its biggest losses in history.

Let's be blunt about this: the idea of buying shares is to make money, and nothing else whatsoever. So before your first deal, rid yourself of any attachment to any company. We know of many people who refuse to buy Manchester United shares because they support Liverpool. Sorry, but if you're one of those, you're in the wrong game. (We're both massive Arsenal fans but have made good money on Spurs shares. If anything, it's been all the more satisfying doing it that way!)

Before choosing that first share, you have to decide how much to spend. As we've shown earlier, with most brokers you can get a decent credit limit of at least £2,000. But it's really not a good idea to go that big. The point of the first deal is really to get familiar with the way the market works. Treat it as a small investment if you like — money you don't expect to get back. It's not worth spending too little though. Some people plough in with £50 — they are already down on their money after broker's charges!

We would suggest going with £500. Now we're not saying you should have £500 spare, because the idea is not to pay for the shares. But even if you picked a real dog and the price collapsed by 50%

before you sold out, the most you would lose is £250.

Making that first deal

It would be nice to think you could double your money on that first deal, but it's best to play safe. Although we've had a bit of a dig at the boring shares — where you have little chance of making very much — it is worth choosing one of these to begin with. At least your chances of losing much are less.

The blue-chip shares we mentioned earlier are the safest bet on the market at any given time. We recommend you go for one of these. British Telecom, for example, is probably one of the safest stocks you could plough into, or BP Amoco. That said, try and go for something that has short-term potential. The areas where the action usually is in blue chips is telecommunications, media and sometimes the food sector. It all depends at what moment in time you decide to make that first deal, so it's hard for us to be specific. We'd suggest that, after studying the papers for two weeks, you have a think about where the action seems to be. If all the talk is about big American companies coming in to take over British supermarkets, then go for the likes of Tesco, Sainsbury's or Safeway. If, on the other hand, the big news is that more people than ever are using mobile phones, pick Vodafone Airtouch or British Telecom.

Once you've decided which sector to go for (the sector that seems to be growing at that moment), look at the prices of all the main companies. Compare their current price to their peak in the last 12 months (this is listed in most papers). If you decided to go for the supermarket sector, and find that Tesco's share price is now at its highest ever, the chances are it will go even higher. But you may find Safeway is at its lowest ever, so you may prefer to back this as a recovery stock.

Let's assume you plump for Safeway, and give your broker a call. The two most important things to ask him are: first, can you do it on a T+ basis, and secondly, what's the spread? Assuming you can, go for a T+10. That's a reasonable amount of time. The spread is the key, though. If the bid price is 250p and the ask price is 300p, forget it. That means the price has to rise 20% before you can make a penny — which is absurd, but not uncommon in some stocks. In which case, try the next best stock. Whatever you choose, make sure the spread is no more than 5%. That gives you a decent chance of making some cash.

Having chosen the share, put the phone down

and have a drink: remember, you haven't actually spent £500. The temptation is to watch the share prices on the Internet for the rest of the day, and if it drops 1p panic and sell out. Don't do that! Most big stocks slip up and down every few minutes as the market adjusts their prices. It's no reflection on what is really happening to the stock.

If you got the shares on a T+10 basis, the most important thing to remember is the day by which you have to settle them. Again, it's shocking how many people get this simple point wrong and end up having to pay for the shares. That's not the point of the exercise — so it's worth making a note of when the time runs out (ask the broker, as the deadline can change with bank holidays and things like that).

Over the next few days, sit back, relax and monitor the share price whenever you can. If something absolutely disastrous happens, like the company announces it may have to close down and the price falls by 50%, then you've been extremely unlucky and will have to pay up the £250. The chances are the price won't do very much on a T+10 basis with a big stock. If it falls slightly, let it fall. Then again, it's worth watching whether the price moves up. Say you get lucky, and there is a reasonable chance you will, and after five days the price is up around 7% — which should mean that after making up the spread and broker's commissions, you should just about be in profit. Assuming nothing spectacular has happened or is about to, we suggest you sell out. The odds are the price is just moving up with the market, for no specific reason. Many people get carried away when this happens, thinking their ship has come in. Most then find that by the time it comes to sell the shares, the price is back down again and they have lost out.

So, if at anytime during your T+10 period you are in a small profit, get rid of the shares. Within a few days, you'll get a cheque for a few quid. OK, it's nothing incredible, but it means you have learnt the basic rule to kick off with: don't actually pay for the shares. You'll have also got familiar with spreads, and your broker should by now be on first-name terms with you.

If you follow the basic steps above, you should make or lose a few quid over the T+10 period. But more importantly, you are starting to get the hang of things. Some investors think they can go piling in, and before they know it they have lost a fortune. If you made some money on that first deal, then try it again with a company in a different sector. Again, don't get carried away and limit your purchase to £500. The biggest mistake, which many people make, is having made a profit on the first deal, to double the stake to £1,000 on the second one. That is financial suicide.

You have to be patient in this game. It's probably taken you a month by now to find out more about the City and get a broker. Spend another month doing the following: over the next three weeks, try a punt in three more big companies and see how you get on. The aim of this is not to make money — but to get familiar with the City. If you choose different sectors each time, such as media, telecommunications and transport, you'll also find you're becoming familiar with the companies in those fields. Before you know it, you'll have developed a reasonably good knowledge of what's going on in the City, and found the financial websites you like best. Believe us, four weeks is all it takes. Don't try and become an expert — but be an expert in the basics.

Should you make that second deal?

We're getting close to the part where we start going through the various share sectors again, and how to spot good companies in each one. But before heading there, having completed your first deal, you have to make one big decision: is it worth carrying on?

That may sound a stupid question, seeing as

you've taken the trouble to spend the money on the shares (and this book!), but it is important. What you have to decide now is whether share dealing is really for you. In our experience, the people who lose the most money on shares are not the ones with the least common sense, or the least financial judgement. They are just not into shares.

So how do you know? It's quite easy: did you enjoy yourself? If so, the stock market is the right place for you. If, however, you spent the last few days fretting over whether you should have backed a different company for your first deal, and tossing and turning all night wondering what the share price will be in the morning, it's time to quit now.

We've come across many very able private investors who lose out each time because they take it far too seriously, and panic as a result. It's a serious business, but the more worked up you get the more you lose.

If you had a laugh, then let's try to make some serious cash.

CHAPTER FOUR

TRICKS OF THE TRADE

Now it's time to get serious. We would hope by this stage you've found out the basics about how the City works, and had the odd punt yourself. Made any money? Congratulations. You've done a damn sight better than we ever managed when we started out. Our first four investments all ended in losses, and we made all the mistakes we told you not to.

But hey, now is when it really matters. There are various ways to pick shares, and most experts would disapprove of our methods. But the test is in the cheque in the post: if it's big enough, something must be working somewhere. Later we'll come on to more expert techniques to really get you going, but for this chapter, we want to take you through our tried and tested ways of making reasonably good cash without too much effort. It is possible — and as we keep saying, we are last people you would expect to have any serious financial knowledge.

The key to picking shares when you first get started is getting ahead of the game. When big news breaks and share prices rise as a result, the problem is everyone and his brother knows about it. By the time you get in on the action, about a million other people already have. It's not even a case of what you know, because ultimately everyone knows the same things. It's what you know before the majority of other people. Those are the shares that you can make good money on.

The other important factor is timing. What you know before everyone else will soon be known anyway, so you have to act quickly. Thirty minutes can be the difference between doubling your money and losing half of it.

Our initial techniques are based on some of the types of shares we talked about earlier: penny shares, recovery stocks and growth stocks. Those are the three you can get a good return on. But, as we have to keep saying, this is a risky business. To make serious cash, you run the risk of getting it seriously wrong.

Making good money from the worst companies

This is our favourite technique, purely because it is such a neat two-finger gesture to the rest of the City — but works so often. To use it, all you need is access to the Internet (or some other means of getting live share prices each day).

On most financial websites, you should be able to find a section called 'Top winners and top losers'. The headlines vary from site to site, but all cover the same information: a list of the top ten performing shares of the day, as it progresses, and the worst performing ten.

These are usually listed in percentage order: for example, on the winners list, you will see the company with the biggest percentage rise in its share price during the day, followed by the next nine. The companies on this list vary each day — if not each hour. On a typical day, the chances are you'll find a couple of well-known companies such as Amstrad, which may have just launched a new product the City really likes. If something big has happened, like Manchester United receiving a takeover approach, you can be sure to find its shares there too.

To get on the list, a company normally needs to see its price rise by at least 15% on the day — with the top company often rising by 40% to 50%. There are, of course, no rules. A company could see its price rise 60% and not make the list, because loads of other companies just happen to have done even better that day. This list is studied constantly by many private investors, who then decide whether they should get in on the action as the share prices keep rising.

What we do, however, is the complete opposite: look at the list of worst performing companies. Just like the winners, the drop in companies' share prices generally varies from between 15% to 50% on an average day. What everyone forgets is that as these prices are tumbling, no-one is likely to buy the shares on that particular day. So they are dirt cheap.

But the key thing is, why are the prices tumbling? Because in most cases, when a price collapses one day, it often recovers the next, because the City realises its reaction the day before was hysterical. That may sound obvious, but it's something that's overlooked by many private investors. The trick here is to look behind the collapse in the share price and find out why it's happened. On most days, at least half the companies in that list have seen the share price drop for no specific reason: it could be a major investor selling shares, or a downturn in the sector. The other half probably do have specific reasons, like a bad set of results, a profits warning, or the resignation of a chief executive. ✓

Let's take a couple of real examples. A company called Electronics Boutique, which mostly sells computer games for Sony Playstations, put out a statement in the middle of 1999 saying that its profits for the year were going to be really bad. Not surprisingly, the share price plunged (as it always does on such statements).

But in this case, it went spiralling down, from around 70p to 35p in the space of a few hours. Once people start selling shares, the rest of the market follows, and it can get out of control — as it did in this case. ✓

That said, the fact that the company wasn't going to do as well as it expected does not justify losing half its value on the stock market in one day. More importantly, the fact that the price is now so low means that a rival company may try and take it over at this lower price. ✓

And even more importantly, the chances are that the very next day many investors will see this incredibly low price as a good time to buy the shares. By about 4pm on that particular day, the price had dipped to its all-time low of 35p — with half an hour to go before the stock market closed. Electronics Boutique was leading the table of 'losers of the day', being slated by the so-called experts as a company in deep trouble.

It probably was — but who cares! Intuition told us that common sense would prevail and this was the time to grab some shares. Before the market closed. So we took a punt of £5,000 on the shares on a T+5 basis. This is usually the shortest settlement time you can get, but well worth it on shares you don't plan to hang on to for more than a day. Our hope was that the price would recover a reasonable amount the very next day. And it did, rising 10% by 10am. The £5,000 gamble had netted £400 after charges and the spread, and we sold out.

The other important factor in doing this is knowing when to sell. Because a lot of bad things were still being written about the company, common sense told us the price was unlikely to rise that much. But many people would grab the shares first thing in the morning. Having got in before the rest of the pack, we're sitting on a tidy profit and all thanks to their original pessimism

This technique is not without risk. You could pick a company that is such a disaster area, the shares are only going to fall further the following day and you will be seriously out of pocket. The main thing to do is pick a company where the price has fallen really badly — if it's only dropped 15% on bad news, it may drop more the next day. And it certainly won't rise 15% the following day, so forget it. Look for the company that's doing worst, and that's where you may end up best off.

It isn't just companies that have announced bad news where you can make good money. Many companies on the losers list have done nothing wrong at all — someone has sold a big chunk of shares, and everyone else has followed suit. The price goes down as a result. Which means that the very next morning, astute investors will see this share as a good bargain and want to get stuck in. But you can be even more astute than them by getting the shares the day before — and let their investment help take the price up. This is often the case with penny shares. Here's another example: a company called Pacific Media, which essentially makes investments in the Internet across Asia. This company had been promising to do some big deal for many months in the latter part of 1999. Each day the price would rise significantly, as rumours spread of a big deal about to be announced. It would make the winners list. The next day, no big deal would be announced (the rumours were usually false). Many private investors would get cold feet and sell out — and the price would collapse, with Pacific Media making the losers list thanks to a fall of between 15% and 20% in its share price. For no real reason. Of course, once the price dropped, the very next day everyone figured this was a good time to buy the shares as they were cheap again — and the price would rise 20%!

It didn't take a rocket scientist to figure out that all you had to do, during the time this was happening, was buy some shares in the company around 4pm on one of the days when the price was plunging. The chances are — and it did happen — the price would go back up by almost 20% the very next day. As long as you were sensible to sell the shares quickly the next morning, you were sitting on a tidy profit once again.

We've given just two real examples. It's difficult to give live ones for the purpose of this book, but whatever is happening in the market, there will always be a list of losers each day. Study it carefully — on financial websites, there should be background information on each company. There is no reason why you can't turn these losers into winners.

Choosing best-performing companies

It's not as much fun, and not as easy, but the same can be done to some extent with the list of winning companies each day. Of course, the trouble is thousands of other private investors are trying to do the same so you are not likely to be ahead of the game.

That said, a lot of people who look at the list only focus on the best performing company. Say they find, for example, Telewest plc on the top of the pile with a 38% rise in its share price by 10am, because of some new cable deal it has signed. They assume that means the company is doing really well — which it is — and so it's time to get some shares. What they forget is that the price has already rocketed by 38%. It is unlikely to go much further, and even if it does, a lot of investors will start selling out to cash in their profits. By the end of the day, the price may only be 30% up on the day. If you bought in at 38%, you will be down on your investment already.

It is better to look more closely at the companies lower down the list, and do so early in the morning (between 8.30am and 9am). Here too you are likely to find companies that have done something positive, but their share price has only risen a relatively small amount: on average 5% to 10%. These are often smaller companies, and the big financial institutions are still considering whether to take a punt. Believe it or not, most of these big guys don't make this decision until 11am when they have their so-called 'coffee meetings'. At this point, they look around at some of the action in the smaller companies, and decide whether to buy some shares. Which means that if you get in before them, you might be onto a winner.

This happens very often with small companies. NewMediaSpark, an Internet investment company, is an example. One morning in 1999, its share price was 8% up by 9am. It had announced some new investment deal. Sure enough, shortly after 11am the big boys decided they wanted to get a piece of the action, and by the end of the day the price was 23% up. If you timed it right, you could have cleared a good 12% on the day. Done on a T+10 basis, and remembering to sell in the same way, you would have banked over £500 by booking £5,000 worth of shares at 9am.

Each day in the City, there is another NewMediaSpark waiting to be hit. The best thing to do is monitor the winners list for a couple of weeks before you dive in. Play with imaginary money and see if you call it right. If by the end of the two weeks you are getting pretty good at spotting the company that is about to make a big jump after 11am, then have a go yourself. There are thousands of people out there who make £1,000 a day doing this — without actually spending a penny of their own money. ✓

But don't limit yourself to small companies. The growth in some companies has been so phenomenal, even FTSE-100 firms have notched up a 20% rise on the day especially in the technology sector. At the time of writing this book, Psion is a good example. In the past week, its shares have risen more than 40%, an amazing amount for a FTSE-100 company. What's even more amazing is that each morning in the past week, Psion has started the day off with a 3–4% rise and carried on, hitting gains of 20% on one day alone. It's been very easy for anyone who noticed to jump on the bandwagon (as we have all week) and make a tidy profit. The trick has been to spot the rise by 9am, and get in. Each day this week we have made over 10% on the shares.

Rotating between winners and losers

As you may have guessed, companies that appear on the winners list one day often pop up on the losers list the following day. Using both lists together — and nothing else — can be very fruitful. As before, you need to spot the companies on the losers list that are going to be winners the following day. However, what is worth doing is going back into a company after you've sold the shares, because it has re-appeared on the losers list.

Each week, you find one or two companies — often well-known companies — that are going through a volatile patch. As a result, each day their shares have either risen spectacularly or dived. If you monitor the movements carefully, you can make a fortune out of one single company by buying when the shares are cheap, and selling when the shares are high.

Marks & Spencer was a good example in 1999, as rumours that the company was about to be taken over would sweep the City each morning. As a result, its share price would rise rapidly. Then, when everyone figured the rumours were false, the price would crash. Timing was crucial here — and this example applies to many other companies that have gone through such volatility for different reasons.

Rumours that Marks & Spencer was being taken over would normally get going first thing in the morning, between 8am and 8.30am. The price would rise about 3% to 4%. This is the time to buy the shares. By 11am, the rumours are being reported on radio and television, and through the afternoon the shares have clocked up gains of 12% to 15%. Not bad for a day's work. By 4pm, the City would start thinking the rumours were false (even though the City was spreading these rumours!). Our technique was always to sell the shares immediately after 4pm and, not surprisingly, the price started falling soon after.

The following day, disappointment that there had been no takeover would set in, and Marks & Spencer would become a star of the losers list. By 4pm the following day, we would snap up the shares again at rock bottom price. The reason? By now, the price is so low that takeover fever would start again. In fact, by 4.15pm the price would start to recover again — and keep soaring until about 4pm the next day, at which time we would sell out again. This went on for over a week, and thousands of lucky investors who spotted it were quids in. Were the rumours true? Who cares! A lot of investors spent hours analysing the takeover prospects, but missed out on a quick buck as a result.

Our advice is to monitor the losers and winners list closely, and look out for companies that are diving between the two each day. They are your targets.

Watching out for announcements

Betting on the top winners and losers of the day is a high-risk strategy, although once you get it right it can be very fruitful. But there are many other completely unconventional methods, whereby you can bank a decent profit in a very short space of time.

Watching company announcements as they happen is another favoured method of ours. As we keep saying, the key is getting in before the rest of the pack. The trouble with company announcements is that they are made officially to the Stock Exchange, usually at 7.30am before the stock market opens, so that everyone has a fair crack at the whip.

Or are they? It would be nice to think you knew exactly what a company was about to announce before it announced it. Unfortunately, that never happens and if it did you would probably get done for insider dealing. However, what many investors overlook is that most major company announcements are planned in advance. The date is set and the market is waiting for this big news — which in many instances will send the share price rising.

In other words, the fact that an announcement is on the cards is already public information. If you get hold of that information, you can then take a view as to whether the announcement is good or bad and deal accordingly. We should stress here that we are not taking about a company's annual results. Everyone knows when they are and it really is pointless trying to deal in shares beforehand because the market reacts in strange ways to results. Sometimes a company can announce a spectacular set of results and the share price collapses — because everyone decides to sell their shares and take a profit, as things will never be so good again. Or, it says it's in a state of complete disarray and the share price rockets, because everyone feels this is the best time to buy the shares. There is no logical format to how results affect a share price, so forget it.

But it's other types of announcement — a new product, a new boss, a new anything. Spotting these companies takes a bit longer, but within a few weeks of reading the business pages you should have a reasonable idea of what is going on. The thing to look for is the smaller companies that are either in trouble, or have been promising to do something positive for a while.

Let's look at a few examples, starting with Dialog, an on-line information company, which had been in financial difficulty for much of 1999. Every other day, the papers would report how the boss, Dan Wagner, was trying to do some new deal with his bankers to restructure the company. The papers also reported regularly how some big new money-spinning deal was in the pipeline. Dan Wagner never denied there was, simply saying, 'You'll have to wait and see.' As time went by, the market got fed up of waiting and the share price slipped to 60p from 150p.

Then, one afternoon in mid-1999, the company called a press conference for the following day, to make a 'series of major announcements'. It announced the fact that it was going to make an announcement at about 12pm the day before. The announcement of the announcement was made to the stock exchange, and appeared on all the financial websites. Even the late editions of the *Evening Standard* carried it.

So what could this announcement be? One of three things: it had done a deal with its bankers to sort things out; it had clinched some big new money-spinning deal; or it was going bust! Generally, if a company is going bust, everyone is talking about it beforehand. You didn't need to be an expert on Dialog's affairs to figure out that it had a couple of problems but nothing serious. Common sense suggested the announcement was either a deal with banks or some new money-spinning deal.

Strangely, as often happens in these cases, the rest of the market waits nervously for the actual announcement to be made the following day. The sensible thing to do was grab £10,000 worth of shares the day before at 60p a go, on a T+10 basis. The announcement came: it was a money-spinning deal with Fujitsu. Just two days later, the shares were 120p. That £10,000 had netted another £10,000. The Dialog example involves being quick off the mark, keeping a close eye on the market, and lots of luck.

Another recent example is technology company Psion, which makes hand-held computers. In late 1998, it announced a press conference for the following day. The company said that at this news conference, it would be joined by other big-name technology companies including Nokia, and Ericsson.

What could this mean? Obviously not bad news. A reasonable guess was that some sort of joint venture was on the cards. The share price was 200p the day before the announcement, and up for grabs. A few lucky investors spotted this gem and piled into the shares. The following day, Psion announced its Symbian joint venture, one of the biggest technology alliances of the decade. The market absolutely loved it and the share price doubled to 400p. Two years later, still on the back of that alliance, the share price had gone to an incredible £75! If you had bought the shares at the right time, you would have made over 3,500% profit in just two years.

In other cases, companies put out news of an announcement weeks in advance, and everyone knows exactly what they will be saying. That may sound too good to be true, and it is. With these, you have to be careful to actual sell your shares BEFORE the announcement. The best recent example is Sir Alan Sugar's Amstrad. In the latter part of 1999, news began to break that Amstrad was about to launch a brand new product (called the em@iler). This was a special type of phone through which you could also send and receive emails. By early 2000, some 'sources' close to the company were already talking about how this could be the best thing Amstrad had ever done.

There was no date for the launch, apart from a vague 'around spring'. But the City began to get steadily excited. Amstrad's shares at the start of 2000 were just 200p. By the beginning of March, they were 300p. Then, in early March, it said the new product would be launched in a glitzy show on March 29. No-one knew exactly what the product was. But common sense suggested it had to be something special, and because the whole market was getting wind of it, now was the time to grab the shares. Sure enough, the price soared to an incredible 600p the day before the launch. The smart investor had more than doubled his money on the anticipation of the launch, before it had even happened.

But most people missed the key to this event: to sell the shares before the actual launch. Put it this way, the company's valuation had literally doubled on anticipation of this event. No matter how great it was, there was no way the price could go much higher. The launch had already been built into the share price. If anything, once the event happened, many people would sell the shares and the price would drop. More worryingly, unless the product was as good as everyone hoped it would be, the price could only fall. As long as you got out just in time, you would have been OK. As it turned out, the City was unimpressed with the event and the price tumbled back to 200p within three days.

News of such events can only be found by monitoring the papers and Internet sites. It is quite often a case of pot luck. What we frequently do is just pull up the share price of 20 companies a day, completely at random. You can do this easily on the Internet, and alongside the price you should find some recent news announcements. Do this every day and you will find yourself stumbling across the odd gem every now and again.

Trading volumes

On many financial websites, you can also find the volume of trades. This is a calculation of how many shares have been traded in each company. Again, like the winners and losers of the day, this can be a good indication of what's happening, or about to happen.

If a lot of shares are being traded in a company, it could mean there is some action around the corner.

Like the winners and losers list, start having a close look at the companies appearing each day. The first thing you will notice is that three or four blue-chip companies are always there, such as Vodafone Airtouch, British Telecom and BP Amoco. They always head up the list, with around 50 million shares a day changing hands. Don't get too excited about this. All that's happening is the big financial institutions are buying and selling shares each day in these companies to try and make some money, just like the rest of us.

It's the smaller companies in the list you should keep an eye out for. If a lot of shares are suddenly being traded, something positive may be on the cards, and it's worth a punt. Take the example of Irish mining company Bula Resources. If you studied the trading volumes list in late 1999, you would find Bula's name popping up on the list every few days, alongside the giants such as Vodafone Airtouch and BT. But Bula's share price was just 3p, and on some days, 20 million shares were changing hands. The price kept creeping up, suggesting something was afoot.

Why? Well, to be perfectly honest, who cares! We'd like to claim the right thing to do is loads of research on Bula, but in our minds, this is a classic gambler's share. We knew virtually nothing about the company, but a lot of people who did know seemed to think something was about to happen. Surprise surprise, just two weeks later the share price was 7p and Bula announced a big tie-up with another oil company. Had you got some Bula shares, you would have more than doubled your money.

The results can be even more spectacular. Arthur Shaw, a company that now specialises in putting rock concerts on the Internet, made a number of appearances on this list, again for no specific reason. Like Bula, its share price was around the 5p mark, and there was a huge volume of trades. Two weeks later, it announced it had signed up several rock stars to get their concerts on the Internet, and the share price soared to an incredible 27p.

With these kind of shares, it's worth asking your broker for a T+15 deal, to give yourself more time for something to happen. If you bet £5,000 on a T+15 with Arthur Shaw, once it appeared on the list, you would have got back £15,000 two weeks later.

Share suspensions

Once in a lifetime, you might be lucky enough to get in on a share suspension. This is the private investor's dream, where it is not unusual to make a 1,000% profit on a deal. It is like winning the lottery, but with a little common sense you can greatly reduce the odds. We've managed once, and everyone we know in the City who has had a go has been lucky at least once, so the odds can't be that bad.

Share suspensions happen when a company is

about to announce something that will have a dramatic effect on the share price. A good example is when a company is poised to renounce a reverse takeover when Stock Exchange rules state the shares have to be suspended. When companies are about to do this, they ask the stock exchange to suspend their shares for a period of time. During this time, no shares can be bought or sold in the company. After a while, and this can be anything from a couple of hours to a few months, the shares are re-listed. On being re-listed, they sometimes open at a much higher price. If you were lucky enough to get the shares just before they were suspended, you could be sitting on a big profit.

One word of warning though: you'll be very lucky to do this on a T+10 basis as shares are normally suspended for a good few weeks before they come back. As you have to pay for the shares, be careful how much you invest because you will need the ready cash.

So how do you find these gems? The best way is similar to the method of trading volumes. Before a share is suspended, word normally gets around the City and everyone is buying like mad! The candidates for share suspension are almost always small companies that nobody has ever heard of. What directors often do is use these as a vehicle to reverse into another company (a takeover of a much bigger enterprise).

This is not as hard to spot as it sounds. The giveaway is that the directors of this small company are well-known people. Take the example of Knutsford in late 1999. Nobody had ever heard of it, but some big City names including former Asda boss Archie Norman, popped up on the board of directors. What would he be doing in a company like this, that has so far done nothing?

At the time, the price was 7p. The volume of trades began steadily increasing, and Knutsford popped up on the top ten trading volumes list. A few rumours began to appear, even in one newspaper the day before. As it turned out, the shares were suddenly suspended at just 7p.

Just one day later, the company re-listed its shares after announcing that Knutsford was going to be used as a vehicle for significant acquisitions in the retail and property sectors. The likes of Marks & Spencer and Safeway were mentioned. The share price re-opened at 250p. Had you spotted Knutsford, you would have made more than 3,000% on your cash in one night. And many people we know did.

Another well-publicised suspension was Blakes Clothing, a little-known Manchester-based clothing company. Towards the end of 1999, the share price began rising rapidly, from 4p to 7p, with millions of shares changing hands. Why on earth were the City boys piling into this company, we asked ourselves.

This had all the makings of a share suspension, and that is exactly what happened a few days later. The shares were re-listed after three weeks with Blakes having transformed itself into an Internet company. The share price was now 200p, so all our mates who piled in at 5p had booked a nice profit of around 4,000%.

Directors' dealings

The shares that company directors buy and sell is another very good indication of what is happening in the market. Under stock exchange rules, there are only certain times when directors can buy or sell shares. And they certainly can't do so with prior knowledge of what is happening in their company, or they would get banged up for insider dealing.

That said, these guys aren't stupid. They may not have specific events in mind, but if a company director has been snapping up shares like they are going out of fashion, then it is a good sign for the future. If he is selling at every available opportunity, it probably means he thinks the company has no future, so it's time to get the hell out.

You can normally find directors' dealings listed in the papers, or on financial websites. This is trickier to make money out of, and you need to keep an eye on it for a while. Generally, try and look out for the smaller companies, where a director is putting a lot of his own cash at stake. If he is prepared to put his money where his mouth is, you should too.

We don't recommend T+10 for this, as the time scale can be much larger. But if you've made a few quid through T+10 deals, it could be worth buying some of these shares long term. And actually pay for them!

CHAPTER FIVE

PICKING SHARES

Let's be straight about this: picking shares is not a science. It's not even an art form. On nine out of ten occasions, picking a good share is down to intuition, judgement, patience and a reasonable amount of luck. Sure, it helps to have all kinds of financial knowledge at your fingertips, and through this book we hope to give you some of the basics. But the basics are all you need.

In the previous chapter, we went through some of our favourite techniques. Using those, it is not unrealistic to bank a good profit without forking out very much cash. As you get more experienced however, it is time to start looking more closely at different sectors — and what companies to look for in these sectors. Just like before, looking out for trading volumes, directors' dealings and percentage losses is a great help. Often it can be all you need to know before making a decision to buy. After all, with a lot of stocks, leaving a decision more than a few minutes can be costly. In this game, if you spend too long deciding, you are probably going to end up missing the boat.

For many of the areas we plan to look at from now on, the T+10 method is still the favoured option, if only because you might get lucky and net a fortune in ten days. However, it is now time to start actually paying for some shares. The trick is to spend very little — no more than £500 to £1,000 — on stocks that within a period of months and years could quadruple in value.

Spotting Internet stocks

As we mentioned earlier, growth stocks are a private investor's dream. In an ideal world, every share you picked would be a growth stock. Of course, spotting them is not easy. The biggest problem is that most stocks are not recognised as growth stocks until they start growing, by which time it is too late to get in on the action.

During the second half of 1999, the stars of the stock market were the small Internet companies that saw their share prices rise an incredible amount, sometimes by over 1,000% in the space of three months. Most of these companies never actually did anything. Investors and the City were just pushing up the share price on the anticipation they might do something in the future. The market for Internet stocks has calmed down, but it still exists. There are still gems out there where you can get such returns.

So how do you find them? One thing many Internet stocks have in common is they did not start out their stock market history as Internet stocks. Most were shell companies, or small companies doing something completely different. And most are listed on the Alternative Investment Market (AIM).

That, as it happens, is the best place to start. On your financial website or in the *Financial Times*, it is worth pulling up on a daily basis the listing of all AIM stocks. Many are well-known companies, with share prices well over 100p. But whenever you do it, you will always notice a handful of companies with share prices less than 10p. These companies are unheard of, and the price rarely moves. Shares in the companies are thinly traded. The question is, what do these companies actually do? It is not a difficult question to answer. All you have to do is get on the phone to the company and ask them! We've tried this a few times, and had staggering success.

Take the example of Pacific Media, a company we've mentioned a few times before. This is a company that, in late 1999, had been sitting on the AIM list for some time, its share price stuck between 2p and 3p. Nobody had heard of it. So we rang up the company's offices, and asked them what they were up to. Very simple, they explained. The firm was looking to make some major Internet investments across Asia. In fact, a quick visit to their website said exactly the same. It was hardly a secret, but it was clearly one of the many forgotten companies on the stock exchange.

The next key question was when would these investments be made? They didn't tell us, but pretty soon, we figured. Hopefully within a few weeks. Suddenly, Pacific Media became a hot candidate for a spectacular share price gain. There is one final question to ask in these cases: how much will these investments total? The company reckoned about £200 million. At the time, the market value of the company was only £20 million. Which means that if these investments took place, the company could be worth ten times as much in the space of a few weeks. Or, more to the point, the share price would be worth ten times as much. We told *Mirror* readers about this, and it was no surprise that within a month, Pacific Media's share price had gone from 2p to 17p, as it started to roll out a series of announcements about its investments. That's a jump of 700% for the lucky investors who piled in.

Pacific Media was a classic growth stock that was just waiting to be spotted. It didn't take any great financial knowledge, just intuition. Other similar stocks can be harder to spot, because they are disguised as other companies. But the companies are not trying to hide anything from anyone. All you have to do is look, ask, watch, listen and buy.

MV Sports is another good example of this. Like Pacific Media, it is an AIM-listed stock where a lot of investors made good money. And like Pacific Media, we spotted it simply by looking down the list and noticing that, with a share price of between 1p and 2p for a couple of weeks, nothing seemed to be going on.

A quick check showed that the company was run by David Lloyd, the former tennis star and highly successful businessman. What would he be doing running a tiny company no-one has heard of, that has done nothing so far? That alone would, in our view, be a good enough reason to risk a few hundred quid. After all, Lloyd is not short of cash or ideas. He sold his tennis clubs for several million quid not long ago.

Another quick check (which could be made on any financial website) gave another big clue: Lloyd had been widely reported saying he wanted to move into the Internet, and was looking for a vehicle to do it through. Bingo! This had to be the one. Once again, investors who jumped into MV Sports at that time helped themselves to a good 300% profit, as Lloyd's plans were made public just a few weeks later.

Some Internet stocks are even easier to spot, because of their name. It really can be that simple! Media Content is a company that sat on AIM throughout 1999, although its share price — around 10p during most of 1999 — never seemed to move. The company never made any announcements. The only reason for looking twice at this company was the name 'Media Content'. It sounded to us like a media or Internet stock of some sort. Again, just one phone call was involved here, to ring the company and ask them what they actually did.

Very simple, they explained. They planned to try and put live football on the Internet and hoped to announce something in the latter part of 1999. This was definitely no secret. It was even in their annual report, which they kindly posted to us. Except that no-one else seemed to have discovered this gem of a company. By the latter part of 1999, as they started to make the announcements they'd always said they would, the share price moved to 90p. A jump of 800% in the space of five months.

It isn't just small companies no-one's heard of to look out for when investing in the Internet. As we keep saying, the key is not what you know, but what you know before everyone else. And that crucial information is always publicly available.

This is certainly true of a few big-name companies that have taken the Internet under their belt, totally transforming the company and its share price. Take the case of Viglen, the education software company run by Sir Alan Sugar (and a controversial stock, as some readers may be aware). The company's venture into the Internet was well publicised in February 2000, with Viglen's share price literally doubling overnight on this news. But was it news at all? Absolutely not. In December 1999, the company placed an advertisement in the jobs section of the *Sunday Times*, saying it was looking for a new chief executive to head up an Internet division. At the time, Viglen's share price was around 150p. Many private investors spotted this, and jumped aboard. When Sir Alan Sugar finally made this old news public, the share price soared to 400p!

The moral of the story is to read the job ads in national newspapers. We always do, particular in IT recruitment. Every now and again, you find some reasonably well-known company looking for senior IT staff for Internet-related projects — projects that no-one realised were in the pipeline. Even in this tricky climate, that means the company's share price could be about to rocket.

So far we've looked at Internet stocks that nobody had heard of. These are always the best ones on which you could make serious money. There are, of course, many well-known Internet companies, such as Freeserve and Lastminute.com. We've never been massive fans of investing in these. For starters, they are too big. Everybody has heard of them, and you have absolutely no chance of getting in on the action before the rest of the pack. Remember, the City insitutions will have got their shares at a fraction of the price you will have to pay. Worse still, these companies are too susceptible to what happens in the USA. If technology stocks across the Atlantic take a pounding one afternoon, you can be sure the price of Freeserve is about to take a dive.

There are a few occasions (very few) when it is wise to have a small punt in these firms. And that is precisely when the technology stocks in the USA have taken a battering, and the likes of Freeserve followed suit. If that is the case, and the price of UK companies has dropped for no other reason, there is a good chance they will recover within a few days. But it's a very risky strategy and we personally have never tried it — although many investors claim to have made good money doing just this.

Other Growth Stocks

Due to the volatile nature of Internet stocks, it is impossible to predict how good the market will be, even next week. As we've said above, whatever happens, we believe there will always be some winners out there if you only bother to look. But Internet stocks are just one part of growth stocks. You would be extremely foolish to stick all your cash in that sector, as the chances are you would lose most of it.

The next best thing is other types of growth stocks, and there are plenty of them about. These are normally found, like the Internet, in the technology sector. They are generally small- to medium-sized companies, with share prices of between 20p and 100p. They've been ticking along nicely for a few months, doing a few positive things. They've had a bit of press coverage, and a small number of private investors are already talking about them. The gains you can get on these are rarely as spectacular as those you can achieve on the Internet, but are pretty good all the same. On many such stocks, you could bag a 500% profit within a year. As before, remember that you should be ready to pay for these shares, so if you think you've found a winner, don't get carried away and bet £5,000 on them. These are more investments than bets.

So, once again, the 64-million-dollar question is: how do you find these companies? As always, it's a case of good judgement and common sense. The starting point is to scan, on a regular basis, the companies that exist in those sectors. At the very least, you should know their name. The chances are you won't know some of these companies even exist.

In any given sector, you will always find a host of big players — the well-known blue-chip companies everybody always talks about. But what about the smaller ones? Are they likely to grow into big players themselves?

Another of Sir Alan Sugar's companies, Amstrad, is a good example of this. He effectively re-started Amstrad from scratch a few years ago, and by late 1998, the share price was just 20p. You don't need a great memory to know that back in the Eighties, Amstrad was a billion-pound company, a superstar around the globe. And here was Sir Alan, back in charge of his favourite company. Except this time it was a minnow. A quick scan of what Amstrad was doing in the electronics market would reveal that, at the time (late 1998) it was not up to very much. But there were loads of plans in the pipeline, all readily available for anyone to read if they could be bothered.

Now the judgement factor: this is a guy whose track record is that he took a company from scratch and, over a period of years, turned it into a world-beater. Never mind the detail. The gut feeling is that he would do it again — or at least give it a hell of a go.

Private investors who saw that potential and got in at 20p were sitting on a share price of 600p two years later. As we noted earlier, things went a bit wrong with the launch of his em@iler phone and the share price came back down. But before that happened, a lot of people made seriously good money out of Amstrad. All it took was realising this company existed, and that the share price was extremely low.

Sir Alan Sugar is a good example. Check the list of companies in various sectors, and you are bound to find a few small ones, run by guys who have done big things before. To us, that's enough reason to invest. You could spend hours analysing the figures, but all that really matters is that these guys have done it before and are capable of doing it again. If you find some, stick a couple of hundred quid into them. There's a good chance that it will become £2,000 a year later.

There are, of course, many more ways to spot growth companies rather than just looking at the guys behind it. One of the best is checking out a sector that is really booming. One where sales are shooting through the roof, and everyone involved is talking about a glowing future.

But having found that sector, don't actually invest in it. After all, that's what everyone else is doing. The trick is to find companies related to that sector, the small ones that will benefit as a result. The Pace MicroTechnology example we touched on earlier is a classic example: at the time digital television began to take off in the UK, the market seemed to overlook the related companies that would benefit as a result. While everyone was talking about BSkyB, the real action was in Pace, which makes the set-top decoders needed to watch digital satellite television.

The irony is that BSkyB shares actually suffered because the company subsidises the cost of these boxes. You can pick them up for free from Dixons now — but every time you do, Pace still gets paid for making them. Pace was a real star in 1999, with its shares rocketing 800%.

There are plenty of other similar companies still out there. It's a case of spotting what is 'in' at any given time, and who else will benefit. If it suddenly became the biggest thing ever in Britain to Rollerblade to work, you can be sure investors would be piling into any public companies that sell Rollerblades. We would look out for the companies that make the blades — they are the ones that would benefit more. Or, more likely, the fashion could soon be to ride scooters everywhere (sales were up 77% in 1999). Well, who makes the parts for scooters? Are these companies listed on the stock exchange? If so, they would be the ones to have a punt in.

So far we've looked at mainly technology-related companies. The other growth sector with enormous potential is pharmaceuticals. There are many huge, household names in these, such as GlaxoWellcome. But look more closely, and there are a handful of small companies, all making drugs, trying out new drugs, or selling medical-related products. When these take off, you can get just as good a return as on Internet stocks.

Again, spotting them can be quite easy. Take Medisys, a company that specialises in making retractable needles. Simple enough — needles that automatically retract back into a plastic container after they have been used, and can be easily disposed of. We first noticed this company in mid-1999, again simply by scanning a copy of the *Financial Times*.

It sounded a bit odd — retractable needles. Is there a huge market for that in this country? Apparently not. But a one-minute check on the Internet revealed something very significant: the law in the USA was set to change in 2000, with only retractable needles permitted (to stop drug addicts passing on their needles). Only two companies in America made the needles, and a third — Medisys — had applied for permission to do so.

Without doing any calculations whatsoever, it's safe to say that this is potentially an absolutely massive market. Medisys would only have to get a tiny chunk of it and would be quids in. The shares were 40p when we spotted it. The information was readily available to anyone who looked, and no more than ten minutes' research was required to tell you that this was a company going places. Investors who jumped in then pretty soon doubled their money as the rest of the market caught on to Medisys — even now the experts reckon the share price could go all the way to 500p.

Medisys is an example of a company making products. However, some of the real gems out there make nothing at the moment. They spend all their money on drug trials. Whenever anyone wants to produce a new drug, the laws require years of testing, in many different phases. We'd be lying if we said we knew the rules of drug testing inside out. In fact, we know practically nothing about it. But we do know this: if a company is in the middle of testing a major disease-beating drug, the share price will shoot up if the results are good. There is, of course, a risk of the opposite happening, but it's well worth a bet on these shares. Simply check out the list of pharmaceutical companies, and ring them up. Find out what they are up to and, more crucially, when the results of their tests will be made public.

If you find a company is testing a cancer-beating drug, and in two weeks will publish the results of the first phase of its testing, bung a few hundred quid into the shares. If the tests come up good, as they often do, the share prices of these companies can more than double overnight. There are many cases of such companies going from scratch to being worth over a billion pounds in less than a year.

Finding Recovery Stocks

With the examples above, you stand a good chance of making good money in a short amount of time. How long is down to luck: it could be a day, a few weeks or a few months.

Having got the hang of relatively short-term investments, it's worth exploring areas where you can do just as well, although it can take a bit longer. These are recovery stocks. Again, there is no definition of how long you'll have to wait. You could get very lucky and double your money within a week if you call it just right, but generally you need to sit tight for a good few months. Whatever you do, don't panic.

As we mentioned earlier, recovery stocks are companies that have had a bad time recently, and the share price is in the doldrums. This could be for one of many reasons: disastrous product launches, financial problems, staff problems or competition, for instance.

Our idea of a good recovery stock is one preferably suffering from as many of the above problems as possible. When things get bad, investors panic and pile out. The price comes crashing down and for some time no-one wants to go near these companies. Yet a few months down the line, you can be sure these same stocks will be back up there, being talked about positively. Everyone has forgotten the past problems, and everyone is buying the shares. If you get in at the bottom, you are onto a winner.

These are much easier to spot, as they are generally household names. When things go wrong at smaller companies, not many people hear about them and the price may not suffer as a result. With big firms, any sign of trouble is widely reported, giving private investors a great chance to cash in on their misfortune. You can find these companies in just about any sector. It's easy to do so. Just keep an eye on the papers every day, and even the news, and there is bound to be someone in serious trouble. They are your meal ticket.

The first three things to ask yourself about a company on the ropes are: how bad are things, how much has the share price collapsed and how well known is this company? If things seem disastrous, look further. Is the share price really low? You need to compare the current share price to the high and low in the past year (listed in the *Financial Times* each day and on most financial websites).

The easy mistake to make is that you hear of some big company in trouble, where the shares have fallen 10%. So you think, 'Great, classic recovery stock.' But if the shares are still twice as high as a year before, forget it. The price is already near its peak. It's certainly not going to rise above that after bad news.

The targets are where the price has fallen steadily, sometimes to half the value of just a year ago. The information giant Reuters is a classic case. In late 1999, its share price was around 400p — less than a third of the price just months before. By any estimation, an absolute disaster. Investors were up in arms, and all the company could do was promise that a new strategy was in the pipeline.

But Reuters was a household name. Everyone's heard of it. With the world becoming obsessed with technology, and financial markets growing out of control, nobody seriously believed Reuters had no future. It's just that the City wasn't impressed at that moment in time. In fact, Reuters' only real competition is Bloomberg — and by any measure, Reuters was still way ahead.

Without doing much research into Reuters' problems, it seemed pretty obvious that the City was punishing the company, just because it could. That often happens: big fund managers get fed up with a company not performing and start bad-mouthing it. Investors panic and sell out. But very rarely do the companies stay in trouble. In fact, if you did bother to research Reuters in any depth (which we didn't!), you would have quickly found there was no serious problem at the core businesses.

A number of astute private investors noticed what was going on and grabbed as many shares as they could afford in late 1999. It didn't take long for them to be celebrating. Around three months later, the share price was back to well over 1,000p. The chief executive was a superstar again, and you had trouble finding anyone who remembered how bad things supposedly were just months earlier.

Every day, you will find similar cases. At the time of writing this book, Marks & Spencer's share price is stuck around 250p — less than half the price it was 18 months ago. But this is still one of the world's best-known brands. There's been a lot of talk about poor profits, and many management changes. To us, it has all the makings of a classic recovery stock. If next week it put out figures saying that sales were looking good again, the price would start steadily rising again. Or more likely, with the price so low, someone might make a takeover bid for the company.

If you go for stocks such as Marks & Spencer, the key is not to panic. You might ring up your broker after reading this and find the price is 260p, so you buy some. A week later it has fallen to 220p. What do you do? Unfortunately, most investors would think, 'Oh my God, what a terrible mistake that was' and get the hell out before the price falls further.

You're forgetting that recovery stocks are a long-term game. You are looking for a share price of 500p before you sell, so don't get out as soon as it drops — which it could well do.

On some recovery stocks, the time span can be relatively short. These are in sectors where figures on performance are always coming out, giving people the chance to judge a company several times a year rather than just around the annual results and major events.

Look at British Airways where, again, you could have made very good money pretty quickly — several times over. For much of 1999, the company was plagued by bad press. Everyone put the boot in. To be fair, the figures weren't very good: profits were falling, and passenger numbers dropping. Even the chief executive got the chop in early 2000. But if you monitored the share price, you would notice something very odd: almost every few weeks, it would fluctuate between 280p and as high as 450p. A difference of 60%, in the space of a few weeks, consistently.

What was going on here? Again, we'd be lying if we said we knew for sure. Most likely, the market was driving down the price every time bad news came out, and then buying back the shares when the price was low: this is, after all one of Britain's best-known companies. There is no way it was going to be in serious trouble.

Never mind what the reasons were: as long as you got in around the 280p to 300p mark, there was a good chance of making decent cash within a few weeks. Then selling out near 400p, waiting for the price to fall again and starting the whole process all over again!

In October 1999, we were on a plane with Sir Richard Branson, heading to a party in Chicago to celebrate the launch of Virgin Atlantic's first flight to the city. During the flight, we started discussing precisely this with him. Amazingly, even someone of his calibre hadn't spotted what was going on. At the time of our conversation, the price was 282p. He was convinced it was heading all the way down. So we offered him a bet: that it would hit 400p before it hit 275p. Quite a gamble! He looked bemused: the odds on that happening, to most people, must have been zero. The tycoon happily accepted our bet, and four weeks later paid up. The price touched 280p and then soared all the way back to 400p.

Unfortunately, he would only bet us a fiver. And even then, the cheque was made out to 'City Slickers' so we couldn't even cash it in!

New product spotting

We talked earlier about how to watch out for company announcements. Often these involve the launch of a new product and, as we said, the trick is to get in before the well-publicised official announcement.

That said, there are many new products launched on the market with little or no publicity, which take anything from a few weeks to several months to catch on. Once they do, the market goes crazy and the shares surge. The amazing thing, which many investors completely overlook, is that these products are already out there in the market. It doesn't take much to find them, and judge whether they are a winner.

We'll give an example. In 1998, we were wandering around Harrods' spectacular hi-fi department, admiring the goods we could afford to buy if we wrote a bestselling book. One of the big attractions was a set of flat-panelled loudspeakers for stereo. Basically, they were designed as picture frames, no thicker than a couple of centimetres. To the observer, they looked like a couple of really expensive pictures — except they were top-quality loudspeakers.

What a great idea! You could tell by the number of people gathered round that this was something that struck a chord with the general public. That obvious invention everyone had been waiting for. A quick check on the boxes revealed the company behind it was NXT. No-one had ever heard of them, and their share price was 200p.

This was a winner if ever we saw one. The products have yet to really catch on here, but as we write, NXT has struck licensing deals across the globe. Its share price today? 1,500p — yes, 15 quid!

Come to think of it, Harrods is a pretty good place to spot new products. Wide-screen tellies were there long before they appeared in Dixons. Wander down there and check out the latest mobile phones, personal computers, vacuum cleaners. Anything. If something catches your eye, find out who is behind it and if the shares are listed. If they are not, who are the other companies that might benefit from sales, and are they listed?

Football shares

We mentioned earlier the folly of investing in shares for sentimental reasons. Soccer fans who buy shares in their favourite club are often victims of this. In our view, it's a good way to lose money quickly. Look what happened to Newcastle United when it floated in 1996: thousands of fans subscribed for the shares, fighting to get hold of some. Every expert in the market said it was a bad idea, but that didn't deter over 100,000 die-hard fans from applying for the shares. The unlucky 9,000 fans who got some have lived to regret it. From an opening price of 150p, the price has steadily dropped and is now worth less than half that.

But that doesn't mean you can't make money by investing in soccer shares. The first rule, however, is to forget which team you support. To choose good soccer shares isn't actually that hard. Because so many people have become disillusioned with that sector of the market, many people often overlook what good bargains there can be.

In 1999, BSkyB began its policy of snapping up minority stakes in as many soccer clubs as possible. This gave many clubs a boost but the enthusiasm has died down again. In our experience, there is only one good time to buy soccer shares: towards the end of a season. Not many clubs are listed, so you don't have much of a choice. But look carefully at the promotion tables in each division. At the time of writing this book for example, Charlton Athletic has secured promotion to the Premiership — and £12 million of extra television income as a result. Regardless of whether the club survives in the top flight, this cash is coming to its coffers. A couple of big signings are sure to be on the way. Season ticket sales and merchandise sales will be shooting up. In fact, the only thing that hasn't changed about Charlton is its share price, rarely moving out of the 50p to 60p range. It's a classic case of 'best not to invest in soccer shares'. That's often true, but most investors overlook gift shares like this one.

There are many other example of clubs being promoted, about to be promoted, about to play in a Cup Final or heading for a European place the following season. Without exception, we've always been able to pick a couple of soccer winners towards the end of the season. Try it.

Penny shares

A lot of the shares we've talked about are by their nature penny shares. But as a sector they deserve a good look. For us this is the most exciting type of share because — let's get down to the nitty gritty — it's possible to make a hell of a lot of money in a very short space of time. Of course, if you 'call it' wrong you can lose a lot too, so the key to investing in penny shares is not to invest any more than you can afford to lose.

Putting cash into these companies should be regarded in much the same way as having a bet on the Grand National — if you win you'll win big — but it's a bloody big 'if'. You wouldn't want to punt your life savings on a 20–1 shot, so don't do the same on a penny share.

In the last year we have seen some terrific gains in this sector and there are a great many millionaires out there who have built their fortunes very rapidly by buying into penny shares. Most of the really big risers in the last 12 months have been so-called 'dot commies' — the Internet companies that have listed at 3p and climbed to 50p, often more, in the space of months or days. Using some of the websites listed elsewhere in this book why not check out the share price graphs of companies such as Pacific Media, Media@Invest, Jellyworks, e-xentric, e-capital and Media Content? These are all companies whose shares were available for a few pennies each last year but in each case the shares soared, in some cases to over 100p. Sure, they came hurtling back down again with this spring's market correction, but that's the market for you.

Just imagine buying into a company at 3p, which is perfectly feasible and has been done many times by amateur investors. You stick in £5,000, which gets you around 166,000 shares. One day in the not too distant future this company's shares could be trading at £5 each which means your original investment would have a paper value of over £800,000. How does that sound? You will have a big CGT liability but that's the least of your worries.

The downside is that it's likely your 3p company is a very high-risk company and could go bust, leaving you with a £5,000 headache. That's why you should never put more than you can afford to lose into them. Making money from penny shares is nothing new. At the beginning of the 1980s there were plenty of investors who wanted to follow Mr Midas himself — the charismatic Asil Nadir. Shares in his company, Polly Peck, could be bought for 9p each in 1981 but just three years later they were valued at an eye-popping £35 each. A moderate £1,000 investment would have soared in value to nigh-on £400,000, a whopping profit by anyone's standards.

And Polly Peck isn't unique. There have been a lot of companies whose shares could be bought at under 50p each before they soared to £20 or more. ARM Holdings was a penny share not that long ago, as was Baltimore Technologies and Durlacher. If you had got in when the shares were trading at under 100p you would have made a killing and, let's face it, that's what this business is all about.

What about Glaxo? Now one of the biggest pharmaceutical companies in the world, it wasn't that long ago that the shares could be bought at 2p. Had you put just £1,000 into it at this level you would now be sitting on a nice little nest egg of £1 million. Even these days that gets you a nice house with a bit left over for a fast car.

It might seem bizarre that a share costing no more than a gobstopper could soon have a value that would buy you a passable three-course meal with wine at a decent restaurant if you sold it. But look at the fundamentals and it doesn't appear so strange after all.

Take engineer Invensys. Its core business — founded by the merger of Siebe and BTR — has been around for years and has grown from a stock-market minnow to a Footsie company with a market valuation of over £10 billion. But whatever its chief executive does he won't be able to grow the company at the same rate as a fledgling Baltimore or ARM. This is why a penny share is a completely different prospect. They tend to be both small and relatively young companies — tiddlers hoping to become man-eating sharks. But at the tiddler stage they tend to do one of two things: they fall into obscurity or go bust because they're trying to grow too fast, or they prosper and grow very quickly. Obviously, the trick in investing in penny shares is to catch a company early when it looks like the latter scenario will prevail.

But whether they succeed, or not, is often just a case of PR. Penny share companies can soon have a market value of zilch if there's no-one out there buying the shares. But if there is a certain buzz about the company — ARM is a good example — and it has a strong product, and catches the eye of investors, the sky is the limit. We've seen share prices quadruple in a few days in this situation, making investors, small and large, a packet in the process. A dramatic rise like this is caused because there exists the potential for dramatic profit growth — certainly much bigger than any blue chip could manage. One good performer that we tipped in the autumn of 1999 was reflective ink maker Reflec. Tipped at just 4.5p it wasn't long before the shares were trading at over 30p — a gain of around 600%. These are our kind of numbers.

Penny shares are high-risk, high-reward investments and not for the type of investor who gets worried if his library book is a day late going back. But every portfolio would benefit by having a few penny shares in them. They give you the potential for the sort of investment returns you'll never get if your money is tied up just in blue chips. So come on — live a bit dangerously, fling the wild hoof and have a punt on some penny shares!

Finding them

Where do you start when it comes to trying to pick some winners? You could buy one of a number of penny share guides. Whether they are 'red hot', or not, you often find the pros in the City have got in there before you. Sometimes they spot some terrific companies, but the chances are that a lot of the early value has dissolved by the time you get to hear about them. Of course, picking winners instead of losers is easier said than done, but if you follow a few simple procedures you can significantly reduce your chances of picking a dog.

You can often pick up a few tasty morsels by looking at a company's assets. Have a good look at what it actually owns that gives it asset value. Often with penny shares you can find some real bargains, where the level at which the shares are trading values the company at less than its actual assets.

The techniques we've laid out above apply to penny shares just as much as to other types of shares. The main thing to beware of on penny shares, however, is the spread — the difference between the buying and selling price. Many people get carried away when they see a share priced at 2p, and think it must be dirt cheap. It may well be. But if the spread is 1.5p to 2.0p, it means the shares need to rise 33% before you even get your money back. Which is not exactly a good investment! The other thing to check out is, why are the shares so low? We've talked a lot about making quick decisions on intuition, but penny shares are one area where we do spend a little more time — and we're only talking about ten minutes here — looking behind the figures. The main thing to look for is any news that the company is in big financial trouble, in talks with bankers and may be about to go bust. That may sound obvious, but it never ceases to amaze us how many people still pile into a penny share because they think 1p a share is a great buy — without realising the company has said the previous week it has run out of cash. And if it does go bust, your chances of getting any money back are virtually zero.

Cashing in on a recession

If you really fancy long-term investments and, by long-term we mean over a year, it can be the easiest way to make good money. We'll be honest: such strategies have never been for us, because like most investors we are too impatient. Six months is about as long as we can wait. But that doesn't mean we are right. We'd be the first to admit that we could have done really well playing a longer game, and the people who've taken our advice on that have always come up trumps.

Playing the long game is pretty similar to choosing recovery stocks. You need to look out for companies that are having a rough time, but are set to recover. The only way to be certain of this is taking advantage of the economic cycles. Unlike most recovery stocks, their fortunes depend on the economy rather than their individual performance.

But again, our techniques on this are very unconventional. The received wisdom is that when the economy is booming (as it is at the time of writing), you pile into companies that are benefiting: restaurants, pubs, airlines, luxury goods and so on. That's true enough, but once again, all you are doing is following thousands of other private investors. You should do okay, but no better than sticking your cash in a building society.

Our thinking has always been that boom times are followed by recession. Things have been good for a few years now, but every expert predicts a downturn sooner or later. Take this logic one step further: just as companies prosper in a boom, there are those that prosper during recessions. Which means that right now, they are the bargain shares.

So what are these companies? Well, as always, you just need to do a bit of lateral thinking. If restaurants are the main beneficiaries of a boom, what do we do when times are rough? Get a takeaway. Are there companies who supply takeaway food shops, or are there takeaway food shops themselves listed on the stock market? Check it out.

If there are, their share price won't be doing too much, and now is the time to get in.

Keep going down this route: How many of us bother with cabs in a recession? Not many. We're all reduced to taking public transport. Look at the share prices of companies in this sector, as they will all rise once times get really hard.

If you want to be really cynical, and even by our standards this is cynical, what's the most common thing that happens in a recession? People lose their jobs. As a result, dole queues lengthen and the DSS is overworked with claims. Who supplies the DSS computers, and other systems needed when claims get out of control? Whoever does will be booming once a recession sets in. The message is you can't be emotional when it comes to buying shares. After all, that £200 you invest in a company that supplies DSS computers today may be worth £1,000 when you lose your job in the next recession.

CHAPTER SIX

LOSE LESS, WIN MORE

Good

It would be nice to think that having got the hang of share dealing, and made some money out of it, you can relax and enjoy the winnings. The biggest barrier to that is human nature: once you're on a winning streak (or losing streak for that matter), you can't help yourself. So often, someone rings us up in a state of absolute joy, telling us how they took a £10,000 punt on a share the day before and doubled their money. How their life is now going to change, and how grateful they are for our advice.

We can't bring ourselves to remind them that if

they reinvest it they could still get wiped out by a market crash. To reap the benefits of share dealing, you have to keep a sense of perspective. It's great to make money, and awful to lose it. But before doing either, you have to set your own ground rules, so that if things go well you can enjoy yourself. And more importantly, if things go wrong you don't lose everything you ever had.

Stop loss/Stop gains

This a common technique used by many professional investors, which we highly recommend. As most private investors have full-time jobs, it is impossible to keep a constant eye on the market. And your broker certainly isn't going to ring you telling you the shares are up or down.

But you can decide beforehand. As the name suggests, this is a method whereby, once you've bought shares, you tell the broker in advance when to sell them. Say you grab £1,000 of Belgo shares at 5p a go, in the hope the price is about to rise. You then decide what you really want out of this investment: ideally, to double your money. At the worst case, to lose £300. In which case, you put a stop gain at 10p. As soon as the share hits that price, your broker will sell them for you. Likewise, you put a stop loss at 3.5p. Once the price dips below that, again, he gets rid of them for you. Except this time you end up with a loss of £300.

A lot of investors don't like doing this, for obvious reasons. What if Belgo just announced the biggest restaurant deal in the world and the shares went to 50p? You will have missed out on a £10,000 pay day, getting just a grand profit instead. Likewise, they may slip to 3.5p because of heavy selling by an institutional investors, and announce that great deal the very next day. Not only have you missed out on £10,000, but you've actually lost £300 It's a tough call, we know. Our advice is not to put stop gains and losses on all your shares. You really have to judge what might be happening for yourself. If you are convinced some tin-pot company is about to become a major player in the Internet, you would be foolish to stick a stop gain on it.

If anything, the sensible thing to do is put stop losses on as many shares as possible. It's a horrible feeling when the shares hit that price, because if you hadn't put a stop loss then you could at least live in hope that the share price will recover. But over time, it's the best way forward. If you have stop losses of £200 on ten shares, the very most you could lose is £2,000 — assuming every share you picked was a disaster. Not good, but not disastrous.

Limiting your investments

One of the hardest decisions to make is how many different shares to actually take a punt in. The better you do, the more you buy. And the worse you do, the more you buy in the hope of breaking your losing streak. Before you know it, you can end up with shares in 50 different companies. If that's not bad enough, the chances are you will take your eye off the ball and miss out on a big pay day when one of the shares suddenly shoots up — because you forgot you even had it.

Our experience is that you should never really have an interest in more than 20 different shares at any given time. Even that is quite a large number. Ten to fifteen is more manageable. That's not to say you shouldn't keep looking out for winners. But if you find one, get rid of a couple of shares that aren't doing anything.

It's tempting to just 'leave those there' as you move on to new ones. We strongly suggest you don't. Put a maximum at 20, and if you do cross it, make sure you sell one the same day.

Also, be careful of how much you are actually spending. Share dealing is very similar to gambling, and just as addictive. You might have a good result with a £1,000 punt, and next time make it £2,000.

Before you know it, you are betting £20,000, which is sheer madness. The trouble is, if you give your broker £5,000 to hold in deposit, he will probably let you have £50,000 on credit. Again, sheer madness, but easily done.

The way we've worked is to calculate the absolutely worst case of losing the lot. How much could you really afford to lose? On T+10 deals, you should be prepared to lose 20% on really bad shares — or if you are really unlucky, 50%. The market might crash tomorrow. You just don't know.

Of course, it is all part of the gamble. If you work on losing 20%, then work back and see how much to invest. So if you can only afford to lose £200, never bet more than £1,000 on a stock.

Choosing various sectors

Probably the most important strategy is to spread your investments around different sectors. Again, it is tempting to go big on wherever you think the action is, but you really are asking for trouble if you do that. During 1999, we knew of people who had 20 different shares, all in Internet companies. Then one day in early 2000 some bad news about the Internet came out of the USA, and all Internet stocks fell. These guys were badly hit.

Once you get into share dealing and increase the number of investments, always try for one or two safe stocks. Admittedly, these are really boring investments, but just stick a bit in them. Food companies are probably the safest bet you can go for.

The other thing to look out for is the volatility of the shares you have. Penny shares are where you can make the most gains and, as a result, the biggest losses. Tempting as it is, never have more than a third of all your investments in penny shares or you could get badly burned. There are plenty of small companies out there with high shares, where you are less likely to lose out big time. We totally endorse investing in a large number of small companies — just make sure the share prices of some of these are over 100p.

Short-term punts

Much of our strategy is based on T+10 deals, purely because we don't fancy paying up for shares. It is easy to get carried away though, and end up looking for a winner every day. It just won't happen. Many investors stare at the computer for hours on end, desperately hoping to find a share to buy. Why? You don't have to buy anything. Nobody's forcing you.

A good strategy is to limit yourself to one 'punt' a

week — the share where you really are going completely on a hunch. It's fun, and often pays off — as long as you don't get carried away if you make money, and try and do it again the next day.

Liquidating your entire portfolio

We can never understand people who go on about how much money they have made in shares, when they haven't actually sold the shares. Until you do, you haven't made a penny. A lot of people get carried away with the idea of saying they have all these great investments. What's the point? It's money in someone else's bank account, not yours.

We suggest that every couple of months, if things are looking good, sell the entire portfolio. Bank the profits in a separate account and start again after a short break.

CHAPTER SEVEN
SOURCES OF INFORMATION

As we keep saying, buying shares is a game of judgement and intuition. That's what we've banked on over the years. The tricks and techniques we've gone through so far are all down to that. Some investors believe that you need to do masses of research on every company before deciding to buy a share. Hopefully by now you've realised that isn't the case, at least as far as we're concerned. But not doing research is different to not picking up information, gossip and rumour. In our business, that is crucial.

So where do you find all this? There is no set rule. We've picked up just as good a tip from the guy in the pub as from our broker. In fact, half the time we reckon he got it from the guy in the pub in the first place. With the advent of the Internet, people who thrive on gossip are having the time of their lives, able to push out any rumours they like. Although most are rubbish, it's worth being aware of them, as they do affect share prices. We've often taken a punt on a share knowing full well the rumour we've spotted on the Internet is nonsense, but credible enough for the market to believe and for the share price to rise! The trick is to sell out before everyone else gets wind of the truth.

Much as we don't like the business coverage by most newspapers, they too affect share prices dramatically. However, it's the smaller stories buried in the corner, which many people don't bother reading, where you can cash in most.

Newspapers and magazines

Our favourite daily, in fact the only one we really read a lot, is the business section of the *Independent*. It covers the news pretty much like the rest, but its 'Markets Report' is the best of the lot. This is the one bit in any newspaper that you really should read every day — it tells you where the action was in shares, in terms of big rises and falls, and gives you a pretty good explanation why.

The thing about the *Independent*'s Markets Report is it also takes a special interest in small companies, telling you the rumours surrounding them. It's easier for us because we're journalists, but even we've often made some fast cash by reading that paper. Occasionally, the *Independent* will tell you about some tin-pot company nobody's ever heard of, at 2p a share, that might be planning to get into the Internet. You could have a £1,000 punt on it on a T+10 basis. If the rumour proves correct within that time, you can be certain the price will at least double to 4p. We've done exactly that twice by following the *Independent*, and made £1,000 each time.

For hard news about company and market events you still can't beat the *Financial Times*. It is essential for investors — especially if they're of the armchair kind — to keep in touch with what's happening out there in the market and if you're not interested, or can't be bothered to find out, then you probably shouldn't be reading this book. So start reading the pink 'un as soon as you can for instant results. The more you know about the stock market and what makes companies tick, the greater your chances of calling the right shots and *making* money rather than *losing* it.

The FT is still *the* thing to read in the morning to find out what's happening although the *Mirror* ran it to a close second when *we* were working on it. Whatever you do in the morning you must read the *Financial Times'* Lex column which is always on the back of the main section. Although we prefer the *Independent* as a main read, the Lex column is very influential. If it says a company is going down the pan, the shares always take a dive — and vice versa. Thankfully for the likes of us, Lex only covers big companies, so we're safe from its influence! However, it's well worth keeping an eye on it. We know hundreds of people who have piled into companies on the same day that Lex has advised readers to stay clear of them, and then wondered why the share price has collapsed.

It's just as important to keep an eye on what Lex thinks is a good bet. By the time you've read Lex, it's too late to buy the shares because the price will have already risen. (We have tried getting to the guy who writes it to tell us all in advance in return for £50, but sadly he wouldn't play ball.) But it is still worth knowing this information, so you don't get overexcited and buy the shares — after the market makers have whacked up the price.

The only other daily paper worth bothering with is the *Daily Mail*, which regularly trumps the opposition when it comes to publishing what looks like inside information on big deals and forthcoming bid approaches. We wouldn't bother reading any other daily newspapers. Again, the *Daily Mail* is excellent for those small bits of gossip that are no more than a few lines long. Look out for those short stories. If, by the time you call your broker the price hasn't risen more than 4%, you can often steal a march on the rest of the City, which is busy working out whether or not the story is true. If by about 2pm the share price in the company you backed is up by around 15%, we suggest you sell the shares. That's usually the time when companies put out a statement saying the story in the *Daily Mail* is nonsense, and the share price collapses immediately.

As far as the weekend press goes the *Sunday Times* and the *Sunday Telegraph* are much the same and are both worth following for share tips, interesting features and leaked details of upcoming deals. Edmund Jackson and Luke Johnson are both required reading in the *Sunday Telegraph* because both have a tremendous understanding of the market and access to the very best information, which they sometimes pass on.

The *Financial Mail on Sunday*'s days look to be numbered as a serious rag for investors although the Midas column still carries some weight. *Sunday Business* is on the up and up but, once again, it's gone downhill a bit since we left it! At the time of writing it's the only paper that doesn't carry share tips. To us, that sounds like the editor doesn't believe in his own staff, so why should you believe a word they say?

Of the investor magazines, the only one we like is the newish *Shares* magazine. It is much better than the *Investor's Chronicle*, which seems to have lost its way as a 'must read' for stock-market punters.

For the American market you can't beat the *Wall Street Journal* although for fun we read *Forbes*. It is worth pointing out that you can get the on-line edition of the latter before it is available on the newsstands. But when it comes to the US, we rely heavily on the Internet for our information.

But what does all that information you're bombarded with really mean? Investors, whether they're armchair punters or fund managers from the major institutions, follow each other round like lemmings. There is a definite herd instinct in the stock market, with people buying and selling exactly the same thing at the same time. That is why you must read the financial press. All serious investors read the FT, so if the Lex column trots out a story one morning that Marks & Spencer is still in trouble, and that its true value could be as low as 180p a share, the report soon becomes a self-fulfilling prophecy and the share price takes a dive. If you've got up with the larks and spotted this, and you own a gaggle of shares bought at 250p, you would be best advised to sell them when the market opens. This is what an awful lot of other investors will do and you would be better off if you joined them. You can always buy them back at the lower price when it tumbles and wait for the next bout of bid fever to come along that will send the price straight back to 250p. That's what the market professionals do, so if you do the same you're playing with the big boys.

At the very least you should scan the headlines of the financial pages every day, which will give you some feeling of the state of the market. If all the headlines are predicting a market 'correction', or even a crash, then there will be more sellers than buyers that day. On the other hand if the tone of reports is upbeat, there will be more people buying. It could be a good day to have a punt. Even a quick glance at the front of the FT should give you a very good idea about investor sentiment and how the market is set to react.

Reading Share Prices

We're assuming most investors reading this will already know a bit about the market and what they're looking at when they consider the previous day's share price movements in their daily newspaper. But here's a run-through anyway. Shares are listed according to what the company does, so if you're interested in Amstrad, look under Electricals. If you're looking for Trinity Mirror, you'll need to look under Media. When you look at a list of share prices you will see something like this:

	Price	+/-	High	Low	Vol (000s)	Yield	P/E
Viglen	181	+12	400p	120p	756	4.0	42.1

Going along the line you will see the name of the company is Sir Alan Sugar's technology company Viglen. The share price quoted is 181p, which is the mid-price quoted when the market closed yesterday (so the investor will have to pay something like 183p a share to buy them or receive about 179p a share if he or she sells).

This is very important. Many investors check out

the price in the FT, and start jumping for joy, thinking they have made a few bob overnight. In fact, they are only reading the mid-price. When they come to sell the shares, they may find they have actually made a loss, because of the spread. If you're getting this information from the FT you might also see a 'club' figure next to the company's name. This means the newspaper will send you a free annual report if you phone them to order one.

Next you can see that the Viglen share price rose by 12p the day before. The high (400p) and low (120p) figures give you the range — how high the share price has been and how low it has been in the last 12 months.

The Vol is the volume of trades and you can see that 756,000 Viglen shares changed hands yesterday (and not all were bought by us!).

The purpose of the Yield figure is to help you work out how much income you're likely to get by buying into a particular company. Viglen's Yield is 4%, which means the total pay-out on each share in dividends (after tax has been deducted) = 4% of 181p, roughly 7.2p per share.

On Mondays — because there is no trading on Sundays — you get the market capitalisation, which is the approximate market value of the company. The

P/E ratio is the price-earnings ratio, which gives investors a few clues about how cheap or expensive a share is compared to its rivals. Viglen's is 42.1, which is the number of times the current share price exceeds the company's profits (earnings) per share, which can be distributed as a dividend.

Share tips in newspapers

Apart from hard news and share prices one of the most useful purposes served by the business press is giving out share tips. Every daily newspaper apart from the *Guardian* and the *Star* tells their readers what they consider to be a good buy and what they advise their readers to leave well alone.

The best tipsters are in the Sundays and it's well worth having a look to see what has caught the eye of tipsters in the *Sunday Times*, the *Sunday Telegraph* and the *Financial Mail on Sunday*'s Midas column. You can get a round-up of the tips on Ceefax, Teletext and also by going to www.digitallook.com.

There are also some great tips in *Shares* magazine, while on the Internet we reckon the best tips are to be found on www.uk-invest.co.uk. Just click on 'Gurus' and you'll get all the latest recommendations from some of the best-informed guys (plus Mrs Cohen!) in the market.

Director share dealings

Something else to watch out for in your newspaper is news about which company directors **are** buying and which are selling. Tables of the big**gest b**uys and sell-offs of the week appear in the Saturday *FT* and the Sunday papers. *Shares* magazine has a section devoted to this, as does www.digitallook.com and www.uk-invest.co.uk.

It stands to reason that the executives who know their companies intimately provide clues about the future performance of their companies when they buy and sell. There aren't many examples of directors buying a whopping great tranche of shares just before the share price takes a dive. Likewise, not many executives are known for selling a load just before the price spurts up. So if you spot a director flogging off a whole slug of shares in a company that you too hold shares in, then it could pay to do the same. If he isn't confident, then why the hell should you be? But if you see some honcho have a massive punt on his own company then, likewise, it could pay to follow him or her onto the share register.

As we write this we've just noticed that the boss of the high-street retail company Arcadia Group has helped himself to over 650,000 shares in his company at around the 50p mark. As the shares have come down from 500p two years ago and the boss himself is currently in the middle of implementing a rationalisation programme, we too believe a definite buying opportunity exists. So we're piling in! We believe a lot of private investors will take a closer look at this company with a view to jumping on board the bandwagon to get a slice of the action themselves.

Incoming results

One of the most important things to look out for is company results. All serious newspapers alert investors about which companies are due to report finals (annual results) and interims (usually six-monthly results). Some publications, quoting analysts' forecasts, also tell you what they expect the results to come in at and what the Earnings Per Share (EPS) are likely to be. Watch closely the share prices of any companies due to report soon. If there are a lot of sellers and the price drops before the results come out the chances are they're not going to be that hot. But a price rise before the results are published is often followed up by further gains once they're out. Results are a closely guarded secret because they are market sensitive, but City analysts are so good at forecasting them that there are rarely any surprises.

However, don't expect to make a fortune by guessing correctly a company's results. Quite often, a big company will announce it has made huge profits but the share price drops, because everyone reckons it's time to cash in their chips.

So reading the financial press is absolutely vital if you want to get to know the market. After a while you will be familiar with the companies — certainly you'll need to acquaint yourself with each member of the FTSE 100 index. Read the headlines, monitor the share prices of all the companies in your favourite sector, follow the share tips and directors' share dealings, anticipate company results and you will find that the City will become less of an enigma. Once this has been accomplished, you can use it to your own advantage and end up playing the thing as though it was a violin and you an expert fiddler.

Bulletin boards

Never before in the history of the stock market has so much information been available to investors. The really good news is that most of what an investor needs before he or she makes up their mind about whether to buy the shares, or not as is more usually the case, is available free on the Internet. But the bad news is that there is a lot of duff information too, so it is essential for would-be investors to separate what is useful from what is a complete waste of time.

The investor is bombarded with information and most of it is completely free. Almost every Internet site now has a bulletin board, on which users can exchange gossip and information. This has become like a drug to many investors, who log on at 5am and sit there for the next 15 hours writing and swapping rubbish. We strongly advise you don't fall into this trap. The easy way to ensure that is never post any message on them yourself. Because the moment you do, hundreds of other people will start replying, and before you know it you too will have become an addict.

Sometimes it's worth having a good look at the boards if you just want a bit of a laugh. Once we saw one BB member ask another: 'Who are these Phillips & Drew people we keep hearing about?'. The amateurish reply was: 'Weren't they two of the policemen from Trumpton?'.

Until recently, there was nowhere a stock-market punter could go to chat about his or her latest investment idea. Now a whole new community of investors is just a few mouse clicks away.

When the share price of Marks & Spencer rises

on bid speculation and falls back sharply on release of the latest numbers, there are thousands of investors who are experiencing the correspondent emotional highs and lows and who want to share that experience with fellow investors. The Net lets them do it, and it can be fascinating watching the boards when something big happens. If that makes us cybergeeks, or just plain old Netheads, then so be it.

The concept of bulletin boards is nothing new. Back in the seventeenth century coffee houses started springing up and bulletin boards are their modern-day equivalent. Those were such a hotbed of business gossip that they spawned the London Stock Exchange. Money is a language that everybody understands and investors have always loved a good gossip about their portfolio, so now the Internet gives them a quick and easy way of doing it.

It is all too easy to take these online comments with a pinch of salt and dismiss them as the mindless ramblings of Net nerds. But sometimes these comments should be taken very seriously. These messages are increasingly creating dramatic swings in the value of companies, especially those of relatively small technology stocks, so following them can give you a competitive advantage.

One of the most popular boards concerns

Internet company Pacific Media and it is largely down to us. As we said earlier, we tipped the company in our column at 2.4p, saying there was a deal coming that would dramatically boost the share price. The tip caused thousands of people to visit the Pacific Media bulletin board on the iii.co.uk website to swap information about the stock.

The rumoured deal and further hype on the bulletin board caused a frenzy of buying and the Pacific Media share price shot up by over 500% over the course of ten days before the deal was announced. There is no doubt that a good proportion of the new shareholders were logging onto the iii bulletin board too. We were written about on the boards as if we were some kind of gods for having alerted investors to the rumours about the deal.

But that didn't last long. Love turns to hate in the time it takes an investor to call his broker to instruct him to sell. When the Pacific Media share price topped 15p a couple of months after the original tip, we sounded a note of caution in our column and suggested that investors might like to take profits and sell some shares. We pointed out that the share price of the fledgling Internet company gave Pacific Media a market value of £200 million and that this was a company that hadn't really done anything yet. It certainly hadn't delivered any profits to shareholders.

As a consequence of us sounding the note of caution, Pacific Media's share price dropped by around 25% (to about 12p) and where we had supporters on the bulletin boards, now we had detractors. In fact, that is something of an understatement. There were people using the Internet to spread terrible lies about us, giving our home addresses and phone numbers and urging other Pacific Media investors to write to us to tell us how wrong we were to advise people to sell the stock.

Along with Pacific Media, another bulletin board favourite is business information group Dialog, which is talked about almost on an hourly basis. Last year, a false rumour on a bulletin board about the group facing debt-restructuring problems sent the shares tumbling by 7%. More recently, Dialog's shares rose 8% in one day on persistent Internet rumours that it was going to float one of its subsidiaries on the US's Nasdaq market.

It is not just small companies that are talked about. Multi-billion-pound deals, such as NatWest's bid for Legal & General, Bank of Scotland's bid for

NatWest or bus and train group Stagecoach's acquisition of Coach USA, were revealed on bulletin boards before the deals were officially announced. There is no doubt that some of the information comes from genuine insiders, so it is likely that UK regulators will try to stamp them out.

We wouldn't be at all surprised if the Financial Services Authority has a go at trying to regulate them, but how they would do it we have no idea, since the whole basis for their popularity is that they're anonymous. Trying to find out who 'darth trader', 'golfball' and 'BigBoy' are would be virtually impossible, especially as most of these users have several identities and adopt different personas for different situations.

In many ways these bulletin boards replicate the rhythm and beat of the modern stock market. News and information is swapped, talked about and acted upon fast. And it is not just the novice investors that play along to the tune — the bulletin board band includes many serious investors and City dealers.

Just as you should not put your life savings on a horseracing tip from a stranger in a pub, you should not stake everything on a bulletin board whisper. Nevertheless, for the careful investor who is willing to spend time separating the wheat from the chaff, bulletin boards can prove to be a source of some very valuable information. The key is spotting it. As always, it's a judgement call. If information posted on the board looks very detailed, it may be worth following up. Then again, keep an eye out for so-called 'rampers'. These are guys who post positive messages about companies, in the hope other investors will believe them and buy the shares. They have already piled in beforehand, and are hoping to make a killing thanks to you.

There's no easy way to spot a ramper. Having said that, you could play the ramper at his own game. If you spot a rumour that looks untrue but several follow-up messages seem to believe it, than have a small punt on the shares. Just remember to sell them within a few hours as the price is bound to come tumbling down again.

Internet sites

While compiling this book we visited a great number of Internet sites for investors — some more useful than others. On a daily basis for monitoring goings-on in the market, checking live share prices and the value of our portfolios, plus looking at the action on the bulletin boards, the sites we are irresistibly drawn to are:

UK Invest (uk-invest.com): A fantastic array of different pundits from Evil Knevil to Mrs Cohen have been lined up to tip companies and give their analysis. You can also get live prices, you can monitor your portfolio and get some of the best research here — and all for nothing.

The Street (thestreet.co.uk): This is one of our favourite sites for news and, again, you can get share prices and informed commentary on market developments. It's free too, although they could start charging soon. The downside of this site is that it covers only big companies, so you very rarely pick up anything too exciting on it.

Interactive Investor International (iii.co.uk): We primarily use this for its bulletin boards, which can be a fantastic source of information. It's very good for personal finance too, and once again it costs nowt.

Digital Look (digitallook.com): We use this to monitor the bulletin boards, get daily updates about directors' share dealings and performance of newspapers' share tips as well as free broker research, which can be indispensable. The best thing about this site is it gives a good round-up of all the share tips in newspapers, and how they are performing.

For more information on a whole range of different subjects, go to the following sites for enlightenment. Out of all the ones we've visited recently, these are the ones we think are best. Remember to put http://www. at the beginning of the following addresses.

Annual reports:
Financial Times: icbinc.com/cgi-bin/ft
CAROL: carol.co.uk
Northcote: northcote.co.uk
Hemmington Scott: hemscott.com

For company profiles and live prices:
Yahoo: finance.uk.yahoo.com
Interactive Investor International: iii.co.uk
Market-Eye: market-eye.co.uk
Hemmington Scott: hemscott.com
UK-Invest: uk-invest.com
E*Trade: research.etrade.co.uk
Datastream: datastream.com
Stock Point: stockpoint.com

Directors' dealings:
Digitallook: digitallook.com
UK-Invest: uk-invest.com

UK Shares: ukshares.com
Investor Ease: investorease.com
Charts:
Interactive Investor International: iii.co.uk
Hemmington Scott: hemscott.com
Trustnet: trustnet.co.uk
Quicken: quicken.com
Datastream: datastream.com
E*Trade: research.etrade.co.uk
UK-Invest: uk-invest.com

Share clubs:
Motley Fool: fool.co.uk
ProShare: proshare.org.uk

Monitoring your portfolio:
Interactive Investor International: iii.co.uk
E*Trade: research.etrade.co.uk
Trustnet: trustnet.co.uk
Quicken: quicken.com

News and research:
UK-Invest: uk-invest.com
Market-Eye: market-eye.co.uk
Bloomberg: bloomberg.com
Yahoo: yahoo.co.uk

Freequotes: freequotes.co.uk

Financial Times: ft.com

E*Trade: research.etrade.co.uk

Financial News Digest: pigeon.co.uk

Performance:

Moneyworld: moneyworld.co.uk

Micropal: micropal.com

Trustnet: trustnet.co.uk

Interactive Investor International: iii.co.uk

Bulletin boards:

DIgital Look: digitallook.com

Market Eye: market-eye.co.uk

Hemmington Scott: hemscott.com

Interactive Investor International: iii.co.uk

E*Trade: research.etrade.co.uk

On line brokers:

Charles Schwab: schwab-worldwide.com

Barclays: barclays-stockbrokers.co.uk

Beeson Gregory: beeson-gregory.co.uk

Cave & Sons: caves.co.uk

DLJdirect: dljdirect.co.uk

E*Trade: etrade.co.uk

Fastrade: fastrade.co.uk

RedM: redm.co.uk
Stocktrade: stocktrade.co.uk
Xest: xest.com

Broker research:
Digital Look: digitallook.com
Equity Development: equity-development.co.uk
UK-Invest: uk-invest.com

Newspapers:
Financial Times: ft.com
Electronic Telegraph: telegraph.co.uk
Evening Standard: thisislondon.co.uk
The Independent: independent.co.uk
The Times: the-times.co.uk
The Sunday Times: sunday-times.co.uk
UK-Invest: uk-invest.com
Reuters: reuters.com
Bloomberg: bloomberg.com

Internet banks:
Alliance & Leicester: alliance-leicester.co.uk
Barclays: barclays.co.uk
Co-op: smile.co.uk
Royal Bank of Scotland: rbos.co.uk
Egg: egg.com

First Direct: firstdirect.co.uk

First-e: first-e.com

Tax information:

Income Tax Calculator: quicktax.co.uk

PriceWaterhouseCoopers: pwcglobal.co.uk

Moneyworld Tax Calculator: moneyworld.co.uk

Chartered Institute of Taxation: tax.org.uk

UK Tax Directory: uktax.demon.co.uk

Motley Fool: fool.co.uk

Endowment policies:

Beale Dobie: bealedobie.co.uk

A1 Policy Shop: endowments.com

Foster & Cranfield: foster-and-cranfield.co.uk

The Policy Trading Company: policytrading.co.uk

Motley Fool: fool.co.uk

Unit trusts/Investment trusts:

Interactive Investor International: iii.co.uk

UK-Invest: uk-invest.com

Micropal: micropal.com

This is Money: thisismoney.com

MoneyWorld: moneyworld.co.uk

CHAPTER EIGHT
TRADING ON LINE

For the sheer adrenaline rush, there is nothing quite like having a big plunge on a company and watching its progress over the course of the next few minutes, hours and days. Heck, there are even a few examples of us clinging onto a company's shares for a few months.

The beauty of all the technology available now is that even an armchair investor can keep tabs on the performance of his or her portfolio every few minutes if they really want to. The technology also means it has become much less expensive to trade than it used to be. If you know what you want to buy, it has become dirt cheap to use the Internet for dealing. There you are, sitting at your computer screen, contemplating which share you should buy next. Will it be a Footsie share? Or a TechMark one? Or how about a small cap share? Or even the classic Slicker stock — a penny share?

Luckily, the days when you were forced to deal through some crusty old broking firm that charged you exorbitant rates for a service you didn't need seem to be on the way out. Every now and again we chance upon the odd broker who will charge you a whopping 2% commission, or sometimes more, on your purchase. Throw in capital gains tax, stamp duty and some other shocking little 'miscellaneous' fees and you can see how it can become unprofitable to trade. The sharks clean up while the poor investor gets hammered into the ground, but luckily this situation is fast being consigned to history.

As it becomes easier to get information from TV, newspapers and the Internet about what's happening in the marketplace and how individual companies are doing, more and more investors are choosing to take control of their own portfolios. By using execution-only brokers they benefit from cheap dealing rates.

We have talked a lot earlier about dealing through

brokers, and the many advantages. The one disadvantage you can't avoid is the fees. Investors normally contact execution-only brokers by telephone but in the past year the mechanics of execution-only dealing have been transformed by the arrival of Internet-based services. On-line share-dealing is soaring In popularity as investors grow more comfortable with the idea of instructing their stockbroker via the Net.

In the UK there were an estimated 38,000 on-line accounts in October 1999 with the number of private client deals expected to treble to 19% of the total by the end of March 2000 according to the Association of Private Client Investment Managers and Stockbrokers (APCIMS). This means the old style rip-off merchants are fast becoming extinct thanks to the huge proliferation of on-line trading outfits such as Charles Schwab and its host of imitators. These days nothing is easier than buying and selling shares and it is all thanks to the Big 'I'. But the armchair punter has such a bewildering choice of who to deal through that it's worth looking at the choices and the pitfalls.

We can't say this enough: opening an account with an Internet broker really is simple. You just print off the application forms on line, fill them out, sign them and post them by snail mail (they need a real signature) with a cheque, or else wire them the funds from your bank account, which takes a few days.

Some brokers actually require to send you the forms first via snail mail to make sure you are who you say you are and that you are living where you say you do. Within a few days of sending off the forms and wiring the money you will get confirmation that your account is open and you are up and running and able to trade from the comfort of your own sitting room (or garden shed if you prefer), surrounded as it is by half-eaten cheese and pickle sandwiches, coffee-stained mugs and two-month old copies of the *Financial Times*.

The early days of on-line broking, where e-mail merely replaced the telephone as a means of a client contacting a broker, are fading fast. Increasingly, on-line trading means that clients practically execute their own trades on line via the Internet by sending the trade to their brokers' computers, which then check its authenticity, verify the trade and forward it to the stock exchange's computers.

At the beginning of 1998 you could not find an on-line broker in the UK for love nor money. At the beginning of 2000 you cannot move for them. UK on-line brokers offering broking services in the UK include: Charles Schwab, Barclays Stockbrokers, E*Trade, DLJdirect, e-cortal, EPO.com, Fastrade, Infotrade, Halifax, Hargreaves Lansdown, Killik & Co, NatWest Stockbrokers, Redmayne Bentley, ShareXpress, Stocktrade, Torrie & Co, Xest, the Share Centre and TD Waterhouse. There are new services springing up all the time.

For the serious investor, the biggest advance in years has come from real-time dealing services such as those offered by Charles Schwab, DLJdirect, Stocktrade and TD Waterhouse. With these services the investor gains access to real-time prices, meaning up to the second price information on the stock. This is vitally important, because until recently the Internet traders only got delayed prices, by around 15 minutes. So by the time you've bought the shares, the actual price might be hugely different.

If you like what you see, you simply hit a button and your order is routed by the broker straight through the market without human intervention. Once it has been transacted you will receive on-line price confirmation and certainty of price within seconds. The broker will, of course, deduct its commission and stamp duty will be charged at 0.5% on purchases. But because of the efficiencies involved, commissions are amongst the cheapest in the marketplace.

All the services mentioned offer on-line stockbroking facilities, including reviews of portfolios and trading. They are also competitive when it comes to pricing, with fixed charge commissions as low as £15 being levied to get people on board. This direct execution-only business is bigger in the US than it is over here but it is beginning to expand rapidly on this side of the pond. Charles Schwab and DLJdirect offer a free dealing period while others include real-time pricing as part of a package. It's well worth having a look at each individual site to see what extras the broker has thrown in. Don't look just at the cost per trade. Some information provided may be included in an annual fee, more advanced information will cost extra, but you may judge it well worth the price.

While we were writing this, Charles Schwab had a variety of membership levels including access to company news and information provided by Reuters for £10 per month in addition to account management charges of up to £180 per year. E*Trade is another on-line broker we like. Running an account costs £50 per year, which entitles you to use broker research and analysis alongside account management tools, fundamental data and charts. At the time of writing Barclays promises to beat the best market price available at the time of trade in the security through its Price Improver system.

DLJdirect offers company data, market news, free real-time prices and charting facilities. It claims to have harnessed technology so that the on-line investor has the advantage of incredible resources at his or her fingertips, plus the ability to pick and choose the information. They have up-to-the-minute information about the market and individual stocks and shares and they are just a click away from taking immediate advantage of their knowledge to change their portfolio.

Which exchanges are covered?

For now, most of the real-time brokers only permit trading in UK shares — that is, companies listed on either the London Stock Exchange or the Alternative Investment Market (AIM). They do not include the unregulated Ofex exchange for smaller companies with insufficient trading history to qualify for the main exchanges. A few are planning to offer dealing in overseas shares in the future — both DLJdirect and Charles Schwab offer Internet dealing in US shares.

DLJ is also planning to offer a European shares service. Clients of Charles Schwab Europe can trade in US shares — including all companies listed on the New York Stock Exchange and Nasdaq — but you will need $10,000 to open a US dealing account with the broker.

However, while there are now around 20 on-line brokers in the UK market the competition has not yet reached the cut-throat levels found in the US. The costs of trading in the UK have not yet fallen to the amazingly low levels seen in the US, although this could change soon. The costs vary quite considerably from broker to broker, and from service to service. Some brokers offer variable commissions, and others fixed.

Some will charge nothing other than a dealing commission while others will add on additional charges. It can cost from as little as £5 per trade plus 1% commission to £25 per trade and 1.5% commission (remember there is also stamp duty levied on stock trading in the UK, unlike in the US). Be aware that many brokers offer a commission-free introductory period. Before you open an account it is vital to shop around, since this could potentially save you thousands of pounds.

In theory there should be no more waiting

around for telephone calls to be answered and no uncertainty on the price the deal is transacted at. Thanks to the Internet, access to the market is instantaneous so you can act immediately and independently, doing your own research, taking your own decisions and acting on your own instincts, whether right or wrong.

Settlement dates

Settlement is the process of paying or receiving money for your purchases and sales. A few years ago a settlement time of ten working days was the norm but this has been whittled down by the Stock Exchange to five days. Instant settlement is the ultimate goal of the Stock Exchange and lots of deals are cleared in one to three working days.

We talked earlier about the T+10 type of trading we like, and this is available with some Internet brokers. The big advantage of trading on line is that the moment you sell something, the profits are credited to your account immediately, so you can start dealing again (even though you don't actually get the cash for a few days).

Settlement periods do vary from broker to broker: Stocktrade offers next working day settlement, Barclays, Charles Schwab and DLJdirect settle ten working days after the trade and E*Trade settles five working days after the trade date.

Types of account on line

Before electronic share-dealing systems conquered the City, most investors held their shares in paper form, that is, they had a certificate stating that they were the owner of so many shares in such and such a company. Most on-line stockbrokers these days try to encourage their clients to hold their shares electronically, using nominee accounts.

Nominee accounts are companies that hold shares on behalf of one or many investors. They are listed on the company's register as the owner of the shares — but your rights as the beneficial owner are protected under law. However, you will almost certainly lose all contact with the company in which you have bought shares — that means no more company reports or invites to AGMs, so if you want these, check that your stockbroker is willing to supply them at no extra or very little cost.

There is an alternative to the nominee account — sponsored membership of Crest. Crest is the company that runs the computerised settlement system for UK equities. If you become a member of Crest (and the only way to do this is by being sponsored by a stockbroker), it's like being plugged back into the mainframe and your name will once more appear on the company's register. Stocktrade offers investors sponsored membership of Crest. Both Barclays and Redmayne Bentley allow clients to deal over the Internet and remain in paper. Charles Schwab, however, insists on nominee accounts. Most UK brokers do have telephone and postal dealing services alongside their on-line dealing services if you want to sell a share held as a certificate.

US v UK on line

There are several big differences between the US and UK markets for private investors. The US already has several million on-line accounts, which is way ahead of the UK. There is a distinct technology bias in the portfolios of US investors, influenced by the fact that 31% of the US stock market (measured by the S&P500 index) is made up of technology stocks, compared to under 5% of the UK market. The UK's 12 million investors are also unusually focussed on demutualised companies and privatisation stocks. US investors get a better deal overall. For a start, commission rates are much cheaper — as low as $7 a trade compared with £11.99 here. However, increased competition is starting to push prices down. US investors do not have to pay stamp duty on purchases whereas UK investors must fork out an additional 0.5% every time they buy shares.

Margin trading is common in the US, but practically unheard of in the UK. Margin trading is like dealing on credit — once you have poured some money into your account, you can buy shares worth far more than the money you have deposited. UK investors rarely get the same freedoms — stockbrokers claim the average investor simply isn't interested.

A fledgling development in the States that hasn't yet crossed the Atlantic is extended trading hours. In the US, E*Trade has linked up with another provider of electronic dealing services, Instinet, to offer after hours dealing to small investors. So although the NYSE and Nasdaq markets close at 16.00, investors can continue dealing until 18.30. Trades are matched with those of other users on a system known as an electronic communications network (ECN) rather than going through a central market. But extended dealing brings its own problem — illiquidity. Investors who deal at less busy times of the day, say first thing in the morning (the London Stock Exchange now opens for business at 8.00) have come to expect erratic prices and wide spreads. Once a steady stream of traders appears, prices and spreads revert to more normal levels.

Investor security

Investors should not worry unduly about security — stockbrokers have used the highest specification encryption systems to ensure that their firewalls cannot be breached. Don't be careless about security, however — avoid obvious passwords and do not leave them lying around.

In fact, the only problems you are likely to encounter are an inability to access the site just at the moment you want to deal and sending an instruction that contains an error.

Systems do crash from time to time, or sometimes the provider needs to carry out some major upgrading work. Halifax suffered a damaging security breach at the end of 1999 in which users of its on-line share-dealing service were able to access each other's accounts. Both E*Trade's and Charles Schwab's US operations have encountered major and prolonged system failures from time to time, so ask your stockbroker what alternative facilities they can offer in the event of a systems failure, for example, heavily manned telephone- or fax-based services.

In the UK, E*Trade's boast that it is a pure born and bred Net broker could work against it. If the market crashes and you want to get out fast, remember every Tom, Dick and Jane will be rushing towards the same exit gate, so it might be a good idea to establish a second account with another broker. Just in case. This will only work as a solution if you are prepared beforehand and split your portfolio. If you only deal in paper, you can use different brokers to sell shares but most brokers prefer their clients to use nominee accounts. Once your shares are held electronically at one broker, you could be committed to selling through them, because transferring your nominee holdings into a new account can be time-consuming and expensive.

What if you make a mistake?

If you send an order by mistake, i.e. you change your mind just as your finger presses the go button or you notice that you are purchasing 20,000 shares instead of 2,000, then you could be in real trouble. Always, always double-check your order. If the worst happens then ring up the broker and ask their advice. They may be able to cancel the order. Or you may end up having to pay for an equal and opposite trade to the one you did by mistake — and get saddled with a big commission as a result.

What's the biggest downside?

It all sounds pretty impressive, and for the most part it is. But personally, we haven't yet ventured into on-line trading for a few reasons. Firstly, as we just explained, if you make a mistake by pressing the wrong button and ordering the wrong number of shares, the odds are you are stuck with it. If a broker makes the mistake through telephone dealing, then it is his problem.

Just as bad is the problem of Internet sites crashing. We're big fans of the Net, but how many times does your Internet connection break down? It happens to us all the time. We don't want to be in the position of trying to make a deal urgently but unable to log on. There is also the problem of overloading. If everyone is trying to buy or sell the same shares, you may have a problem getting through.

In summary, we reckon you should only go on line after you've become familiar with the way the City works — as it's a whole new ball game. True, commissions are higher with traditional brokers, but it's a price worth paying in our opinion.

CHAPTER NINE

TRADING OVERSEAS

Now the world is such a small place and on-line brokers can get you stock in any country where they have a stock market, it is a cinch to buy shares in foreign companies. If you're fed up with the boring old Footsie and want to throw a few quid the way of some terrifically dodgy small cap company you've heard about in Australia promising high returns, then now you can do it. It's a fun idea to consider buying shares overseas. It will not only help to broaden your portfolio, which can help reduce risk, but will also give you the opportunity of making better returns, and teach you about other markets.

Historically, many overseas markets have performed better than the UK and it is tempting to chase these returns. But there's a great gulf between considering overseas stocks and actually buying them. Investing overseas requires greater sophistication because as well as the investment risk, there will be a currency risk. Put simply, the currency risk means that if sterling rises, your foreign investment will be worth less when you come to sell. On the other hand, if sterling falls your investment could be worth more. The risk means that investors need to keep as close an eye on currency movements and speculation as they do on the performance of stock markets and individual companies.

For this reason overseas investment in shares is not for the faint-hearted. If you have any doubts about your ability to cope with the added risk, simply keep your investments in the UK. But as you become more experienced, and develop good market sources, you'll find yourself drawn to foreign markets.

The markets

Before even considering overseas investment, you

need to find out a little about the markets outside the UK. Broadly they can be broken down into three areas: Europe, the US and the rest of the world. Keeping in mind the rule that you should only invest in what you know, then Europe and the US are likely to be most popular to UK investors.

Some may be tempted to other parts of the world, such as the so-called Tiger economies of Southeast Asia. But remember, while returns from these markets can be spectacular, they are more prone to collapse, as the financial crises of October 1997 and 1998 reminded us.

With on-line brokers, it's never been easier to invest in overseas shares — major stockbroking firms will usually offer a service allowing you to buy shares in most major countries. But costs can be up to twice as high as investing in UK markets and there may well be complications because of differences in accounting and regulatory standards overseas.

The US

In the last decade, US stock markets have powered ahead of the rest of the world. Some of the biggest share success stories of recent times — such as Microsoft, Intel and Dell — have started their lives as small stocks on the US electronic exchange Nasdaq, and many overseas investors have been keen to help themselves to a slice of the action. Today, you'll be able to find plenty of commentators advising against US investment, although we reckon careful study of stocks should let you unearth some superb long-term plays both on Nasdaq and on the NYSE.

Europe

There are plenty of blue-chip opportunities in Europe, not least in the motor industry, with respected names such as BMW, Fiat and Volvo. In fact, wherever you look in Europe, there are names familiar to British investors, which should make backing them easier. Now that Britain is part of the EU, you'd expect that investing in Euro-shares would be simple, but that level of harmonization is still some way off.

There is a planned link between London and Frankfurt, which may prove the first step in the creation of a Europe-wide exchange. If this does come to fruition then Euro-shares should be able to be traded using the same settlement system, making dealing easier and cheaper for all.

Rest of the world

There are some great opportunities elsewhere, but

also plenty of opportunities to lose a pile of cash. Some commentators are talking up Japan, but the collapse of that market is still recent enough to put most investors off. Knowledge is power as far as investment is concerned, and this should deter most UK investors away from these more speculative areas.

Even closer to home risks are great, as anyone who invested in the heavily-promoted opportunities supposedly offered by Eastern Europe in the last few years, will testify!

Home or away?

The idea of investing overseas is likely to prove more fun than actually doing so. This is because of the greater risks of investing without enough knowledge and the added risk of currency fluctuations. There is plenty of information on the Internet to give novice investors a head start, but you should be wary of making presumptions and falling for wild claims.

CHAPTER TEN

SPREAD BETTING

One of the best ways to make some fast cash in the City is via the spread bet. Instead of buying the shares of a company, you call a smart City bookie and place a bet on its share price. What a laugh! In the City you can bet on virtually anything with spread-betting firms such as IG Index, City Index and Spreadex offering spreads on a huge number of different financial markets.

To open a spread-betting account, the punter is asked to provide proof of a certain level of assets, dependent on the desired credit limit. All bets are taken over the telephone and at the end of every dealing period there will be either a cheque or, if you screw up, a large bill.

Say you reckon the Footsie will put on 300 points this week, or the dollar is going to plummet against the pound, or you reckon there's some bad news on the way about British Airways and the price will go into freefall. Each scenario could potentially make you a small fortune in a matter of days if you're right. But if you're wrong you could just as easily lose a fortune, so if you're averse to risk, spread betting ain't the game for you.

There is a craze for this type of gambling in the Square Mile and some City bigwigs have lines of credit extending to over £1 million with the spread-betting firms. One fund manager we know lost over £3 million to a spread-betting firm recently in the course of six months by betting on a market crash that never materialised. It shows how easy it is to get your fingers burnt, even if you're supposed to know what you're doing.

Someone else known to us who had never worked in the City before, and who was completely new to the world of spread betting, made over £5 million in 12 months by betting on the foreign exchange markets. He kept on re-investing his winnings, plonking more and more on, and calling the market right every time. What luck — £5 million and it's all free of tax.

We have had mixed success with spread betting. When the retailers got a good kicking on the market in 1999, Boots' share prices took a dive and we had a big bet on it to recover much of the lost ground very quickly. Unfortunately for the Slickers the damn share price did a Titanic and we lost a packet when we were forced to close out the bet.

But we got it all back and more on Psion. We had a hunch that the share price of David Potter's superb company — the one that makes those personal organisers — would continue to rise and rise due to investors' seemingly limitless appetite for tech stocks.

But it is not just financial markets the City boys love to have a punt on — most of them love betting on sports too, primarily golf, cricket and football. During Euro 96, two of the best-known spread firms — IG Index and City Index — reported a huge increase in business, which peaked on the Friday before England knocked out Spain in a penalty shoot-out. Correspondingly, trading in London's financial centre grew quiet on that Friday afternoon as attention switched from bonds to betting. Brokers even feared that a bad result for England would have created trouble in the markets on Monday. 'If England go out, expect gilts to be down half a point on Monday,' we remember one futures broker telling us.

This is a game where you have to take the rough with the smooth. There is no point getting dispirited if you get it very badly wrong. If you're fearless enough you will bounce back. The best bit about spread betting is that it's a tax-efficient alternative to conventional dealing in futures markets, stock markets and currencies. You can make substantial profits by backing your judgement in financial markets. There are dozens of different bets to choose from. The rewards can be considerable, and unlike profits from orthodox share dealing, all profits are for the moment free from UK capital gains and income tax. Every penny of profit is yours to keep. Of course, trading financial markets can result in large losses as well as large profits, and the Slickers strongly recommend that you only have a punt with money you can afford to lose.

So how does it work?
Although it takes some explaining, spread betting is gripping and adds excitement to any financial market

or sport if you're having a punt. But it is highly volatile and the winners become ever more successful, while losing hits the pocket harder than ever.

The spread-betting firms do not quote odds like conventional high street bookies. They all quote 'spreads' and all work in basically the same way. They make a quote for the price of a market at some date in the future, for example, the FTSE 100 Index in December. You decide whether the market will be higher or lower than their quote by that time. If you think it will be higher, you make an 'Up Bet', in other words you 'buy' at the spread-betting firm's quote. If you think it will be lower you make a 'Down Bet' and 'sell' at their quote.

The great thing about spread betting is that you can take your profit (or cut your losses) at any time — you do not have to wait for your bet to expire. On a 'buy' bet you close by 'selling' at the current quote. On a 'sell' bet you close by 'buying' at the current quote. Each move cancels out the original bet.

Suppose it is June and you want to place a bet on the direction of the Footsie over the coming three months. You call your spread firm and ask for its price for the September FTSE. They quote you

6450–6460. This means you can 'buy' at 6460 or 'sell' at 6450 (all 'buy' transactions are made at the top end of the spread and all 'sells' at the lower end).

You decide the market is going to fall, so you 'sell'. You decide to risk £5 per point so you sell £5/point at 6450. Then one of a few things can happen and you have to decide what you're going to do. The market rises in July and you decide to cut your losses. You phone up your spread-betting firm for their current September FTSE price. They quote 6550–6560. Remember, to close a 'sell' bet you tell the dealer you want to 'buy'.

Your loss is calculated as follows:

Closing price: 6560
Opening price: 6450
Difference: 110
You lose 110 x £5 = £550
(What a bummer — better luck next time.)

However, maybe you called it right. Say you had correctly forecast that the market was going to rise. Instead of 'selling' you 'bought' the original September FTSE at 6460 at £5 per point. Once again, with the market looking so buoyant in July you phone up your spread-betting firm for their current

September FTSE price so that you can take the profits. They quote 6550–6560. Remember, to close a 'buy' bet you tell the dealer you want to 'sell'.

Your win is calculated as follows:

Closing price: 6550
Opening price: 6460
Difference: 90
You win 90 x £5 = £450 (And it's tax free.)

However, instead of closing the bet you could have let it run to expiry in September. Had the market continued to rise in July and August you would now be sitting on quite a nice slush fund if you had 'bought' the original September FTSE.

But had you 'sold' the original September Footsie, with the market rising you would have racked up significant losses. Spread betting has been likened to removing a diamond necklace from around a tiger's neck — it can be extremely profitable if you emerge alive with the spoils but there are inherent risks involved.

Or, if you feel more at home with sports rather than financial markets, why not have a punt on the outcome of the winning time in the men's 100m final at the Sydney Olympics? Say the 'spread' quoted by spread-betting firms prior to the race is 9.86 seconds to 9.88 seconds. Punters have two options. If they believe the victor will cross the finishing line in under 9.86 seconds, they 'sell' at 9.86. If they believe he will take longer than 9.88 seconds to win the race, they 'buy' at 9.88. The two-point 'spread' between the two figures is the bookie's profit margin.

Imagine a punter who feels lucky and 'buys' at £10 a point. Every hundredth of second it takes the winner beyond 9.88 seconds to win the race will earn him £10. So if Ato Boulden trots in first at 10.03 seconds, that punter would be £150 better off. Similarly, the punter loses £10 for every hundredth of a second below 9.86 clocked up by the victor so he would incur losses of £160 if the winning time is a record-breaking 9.70.

The golden rule of spread betting is that you need to be aware all the times that it's possible to make substantial losses as well as substantial profits when you bet in this way. That's why you need to know about the mechanisms for limiting your losses. All the big spread firms offer limited-risk bets that allow you to put an absolute ceiling on your maximum possible loss without affecting your ability to make potentially unlimited profits.

Controlled Risk bets

With this sort of bet you specify a level at which you want your bet to be closed (known as the stop-loss, as with shares), should the market move against you. The firm will guarantee your bet will be closed at the chosen level. When you open a bet, you tell the dealer you want it to be a Controlled Risk bet.

Say it is April and you believe that Wall Street will fall in the next two months. You phone your firm and ask for their quote for June Wall Street. They quote 9919–9933. You decide to sell at £15/point but are keen to limit your risk to a maximum £900.

The opening price for a Controlled Risk 'sell' is the middle of their quote minus their controlled risk spread of 18: 9926 minus 18 = 9908. You sell £15/point at 9908. As you want to bet £15 a point, but only risk losing £900, you can only afford the stock to go 60 points against you, in this case up to 9968 from 9908, so you put a Controlled Risk stop at 9968.

In the weeks after opening the bet, Wall Street does fall. Do you want to take your profit? If yes, ask for their current June Wall Street price. They quote 9795–9809.

Your profit is calculated as follows:

Opening price: 9908

Closing price: 9809

Difference: 99

You win 99 × £15 = £1,485 (The drinks are on you!)

However, what if your judgement proves faulty and Wall Street rapidly makes gains? One morning the quote opens at 9985–9999. The middle price of their quote, 9992, is above your stop level of 9968, so your bet is automatically closed out at 9968.

Your loss is calculated as follows:

Closing price: 9968

Opening price: 9908

Difference: 60

You lose 60 × £15 = £900

Golden rules of spread betting

The key rule is to bet early. In order to gain maximum benefit from your speculations in the week and to take advantage of the full movement of the markets it should prove prudent to bet early. The longer you leave it to enter the more accurate the spread-betting firm's spread (prediction) is likely to be as the closing level draws closer. Also remember to close out your bet wisely by limiting losses and taking profits. You should aim to monitor your bets on a daily basis and look to profit or restrict the loss from market movements in the course of the week. The hardest thing to do in spread betting is to realise a loss. Bite the bullet and be brave if you are on the wrong side of the market! Also, selecting your stake is critical. Depending on how confident you feel you should spread your budget accordingly. You should not expose yourself to a liability unless you think it's worth the risk.

Health warning

Just to make it absolutely clear that you need to know what you're doing if you start spread betting, read this next bit as a cautionary tale. It shows the nightmare that awaits those who call the market wrong and stake too highly.

Before Euro 96 began, one punter we know in the market placed a £50 bet, believing the quickest goal would come at 350 seconds or later into any game. Unfortunately for him, Stoichkov scored after 148 seconds in the match between Bulgaria and Romania — 202 seconds sooner than the punter had predicted. Our pal had to write out a cheque for over £10,000. If it happened to him it can happen to you.

Where to find out more information

The best information comes from the spread-betting firms themselves. Our preference is for IG Index (Tel: 020 7896 0000) since that is the firm we have always used ourselves both for betting on financial markets and sports. We have always had very good service although other punters we know in the market favour a newish firm called Financial Spreads (Tel: 020 7332 9400), as well as William Hill Index (an offshoot of the high-street bookie, tel: 0870 518 1715), and Sporting Index (Tel: 020 7820 9780).

CHAPTER ELEVEN

SHARE CLUBS

The hardest part of share dealing is making that decision on your own, and having to live by the consequences all on your own. There is no-one to blame but yourself when it goes wrong. And when you make a killing, no-one wants to celebrate with you because they are all jealous, and bored of your stock-market stories. Which is why, especially if you are an ultra-cautious kind of person, it may be worth joining or setting up a share club as an ideal introduction into the world of stock-market investment.

As the name suggests, share clubs are a group of people who all chip in an agreed amount of cash into the kitty, and agree what shares to spend it on. Because investment decisions have to be made jointly and agreed by club members, group wisdom normally prevails, so reducing the chances of buying into a wildly speculative share. (Which is why we've never been allowed to join any).

Also, because your cash is collectively used to buy shares, it gives you greater purchasing power and reduces the impact of costs. Buying shares costs around £20, with the same charge again when you sell. So if you bought £100 worth of shares, you'd need to see 40% growth just to cover your costs. If there are 20 of you putting £100 towards buying a share, the impact of the £20 dealing charge is clearly much smaller.

Being part of a share club and attending regular meetings can be jolly good fun and give you a much greater understanding of the thrills of investing in shares.

What's the downside?

We have to be honest here. The pair of us have never been attracted to the idea of a share club because most investors would have a heart attack when they heard our share recommendations. And in doing the research for this chapter, it's dawned on us that the administration seems a bit of a nightmare. Unless you get in with a group of people who like that sort of thing, it's bound to go wrong.

The other big problem is, who do you go in with in a share club? The obvious answer is a group of mates who all want to make a bit of cash. But we know many stories where the group has decided to stick a lot of cash into one company because one of the members is convinced it's a winner. Then the price collapses, they all lose their money and fall out. So in other words, it's just not worth doing it with friends, as most times it ends in tears.

You can look around work and other places for more 'professional'-looking clubs. But again, you might end up stuck with a group of people you can't stand, and get really bitter because they are costing you money. It's a tough call. We're not the kind of guys suited to share clubs. But don't get us wrong. Many work very well and make decent cash for the members, so you have to make that decision yourself.

Being part of a share club is supposed to be fun and, hopefully, profitable! But it can easily turn into an administrative nightmare if you do not get yourself, and the other club members, well organised. Here are some handy hints for making sure your club runs smoothly.

Setting up a partnership

Legally, most share clubs are set up as partnerships, which cuts out the expense of forming a limited company and the potential problems of corporation tax. Importantly, the Inland Revenue seems content with this system and has set up a simplified scheme for clubs to make tax returns, providing you conform to guidelines set out in the Proshare Manual. You can call Proshare on 020 7220 1730 for more details.

If you do set up your club as a partnership, you will have to meet certain responsibilities (based on the principle that every partner is responsible for the club's commitments) and limit the number of members in your club to 20.

The Financial Services Act 1986

This Act covers share clubs and there are severe penalties for breaking its rules so it is well worth being aware of its provisions. If you are in any doubt, you should get legal advice.

The Act requires anyone carrying out investment business to be authorised, unless their activities are excluded from its scope. There is a lot of work involved in becoming authorised so you will probably want to avoid it. Members of share clubs are exempt from the provisions of the Act providing they only act on their own, or the club's, behalf, and there is no payment involved.

Clubs must make sure they do not give advice on investments to other people as this would require authorisation. This relates to recommending individual company shares rather than giving general investment advice to other clubs.

Legally, the club's members must have day-to-day control over their investments, so make sure it is run democratically! The arrangement you have with your broker is important here — the Proshare Manual contains guidelines, worked out in conjunction with APCIMs and the SFA, to guide brokers who want to carry out share club business.

Buying shares

This is the exciting part of belonging to a share club and where your regular meetings will become lively as members debate which companies should be bought or sold. There are, however, a few rules you need to be aware of before you start. It is also worth closely investigating different ways of buying and selling shares through a club to make sure you get a good deal.

Keeping account

One of the essential jobs of the club's treasurer is to keep its accounts. This might seem a formidable task but need not be so, even for those with no previous experience.

The two accounting systems commonly used by share clubs are the proportional system and the unit valuation system. To operate the proportional system well, you do need a full understanding of accountancy techniques so, unless one of your members is a qualified accountant, it makes sense to use the unit system, described in detail in the Proshare Manual. In fact, if one of the members is an accountant, we suggest you don't join the club as he or she is bound to bore you to tears.

Running a successful share club is about more than choosing shares. A club needs to build up funds before members can invest, so one of the first things the club's treasurer and chairperson or secretary should do is set up a bank account. Setting up an account shouldn't be difficult, but it does pay to search out the best deals.

A share club's banking needs shouldn't be all that

complicated. Clubs need an account so that members can pay in their subscriptions each month, pay in dividend cheques from the companies you invest in and meet any costs involved in running a club.

As a bare minimum, the account needs to offer a cheque book or on-line or telephone transfers so the club can move funds to its stockbroker in order to buy shares. Ideally, there should be no fees for this; if the account pays interest, so much the better.

Banking rules mean that clubs have to nominate two or three officers as signatories on an account. For security reasons, it might be best to set up an account where two of the three officials have to sign each cheque. Banks and building societies will ask to see the club's minutes of meetings and possibly a copy of its rules or constitution before opening an account, and the signatories will have to provide proof of identity. The process is pretty straightforward: banks and building societies have information packs explaining how to set up an account.

The best account to opt for is one specially designed for a club or society. Banks sometimes call these 'treasurer's accounts'. A club account can have the club's name, and it is relatively easy to change the signatories as members come and go.

Share clubs should watch out for bank charges, and in particular steer clear of business accounts, even if they have a 'free' period. After all, members are paying in money to invest, not to pay the bank. If there is a choice, all but the richest clubs will find that low or no charges are more important than the interest rate.

The high-street banks will be the most convenient place to turn for many clubs. Bank staff are well used to dealing with clubs and societies of all kinds, and there is a good chance that they will know about share clubs.

The four main English clearing banks — Barclays, HSBC (Midland), Lloyds TSB and NatWest — as well as the Royal Bank of Scotland and Bank of Scotland run accounts suitable for clubs. NatWest offers free banking for clubs with turnover under £25,000 a year and Bank of Scotland does so without restriction. Barclays, Lloyds TSB and HSBC offer free accounts but restrict the number of withdrawals each year. Royal Bank of Scotland levies charges. All the banks except NatWest pay interest.

Clubs could also consider Girobank, the cheque account that can be accessed through post offices, where there are no charges but, unfortunately, no interest either.

Keeping check

The bank account you open must be set up in the name of the club but the bank or building society must be given written confirmation, including specimen signatures, of those entitled to draw cheques.

The account number and sort code should be given to all members so they can pay their monthly subscriptions by standing order. Unless you want the hassle of chasing everyone for a cheque every month, having everyone pay by standing order makes sense.

Ask the bank to have your monthly statements made up to the club's valuation day. This will help the treasurer prepare the monthly financial report.

Money on account with a broker

An alternative and straightforward solution is to leave money on deposit with the club's stockbroker. Brokers keep their clients' cash in secure accounts, and the rates of interest will often be considerably higher than at a bank or building society.

Clubs should check whether their chosen broker will accept multiple standing orders, otherwise the money will still need to come through a bank account. Money on deposit with a broker has a number of advantages though: there are no delays transferring funds, and members can check their cash as well as investments over the Internet.

When you have bought shares, you will be issued with a share certificate. But, because it cannot be issued in the name of a partnership (and a share club is regarded as a partnership) you will need to set up a nominee company. These accounts, run by stockbrokers, are becoming more popular with clubs as the shares you buy are automatically registered in the stockbroker's name, eliminating the need for you to set up a limited company.

Nominee accounts have other benefits — paperwork and administration is reduced and dealing is usually easier and cheaper. The broker can also provide regular portfolio information and might also provide a share information service.

Paperwork

It is worth drawing up a formal agreement between your club and its broker. Make sure this is signed by all members. You should give your broker a copy of the club's constitution, plus the names, addresses and telephone numbers of all officers in the club.

An alternative to setting up a nominee account is to appoint two or three club members as trustees and register your investments in their names. But this can be problematic if one trustee leaves — each of the investments registered in that name will have to be re-registered using a stock transfer form. You will have to pay stamp duty of 0.5% and there might also be a company registration fee.

Tax and your club

All of us must declare any income or gains we make from shares to the Inland Revenue. And, unfortunately, it applies as equally to profits made through share clubs as it does through individual shareholdings. Share clubs are regarded as partnerships under which each member is required to declare their own share of the profits on individual tax returns.

There are two different taxes that you need to be aware of: capital gains tax — which is levied on your profits, and income tax — which is levied on dividends and other share income.

What you need to do

You should notify the nearest Inland Revenue office of the existence of your club. It's a good idea for the club treasurer to talk to someone in the tax office about club tax and get the necessary forms.

Share clubs come under one of three categories for tax purposes: clubs that qualify under the 'simplified scheme'; clubs that operate under the 'standard form of agreement'; or clubs outside these schemes that must fall into line with strict statutory requirements. The latter really only applies to clubs with more than 20 members, which should have professional advisers to deal with the tax authorities.

The simplified scheme

This is the easier option. To qualify, clubs must not have more than 20 members; subscriptions must be no higher than £1,000 per member each year; net gains must not be more than £5,000 for the club in a year; average investment per person based on cost price must not be more than £5,000; and members must agree each year how to apportion the capital gains tax liability.

You'll need to complete forms 185-1 and 185-2, which should be available at your local tax office. Of course, with tax returns nothing is that easy, and the club treasurer will probably have to pull out a calculator to work out how to apportion gains and income to each member, especially if people are making different monthly contributions. It may not sound that simple but it's a doddle compared with the complications of the alternative.

Standard form of agreement
After a year or two, any successful share club will fall foul of the conditions laid down for the simplified scheme, hopefully because net gains stampede through the £5,000 barrier! When this happens, the club will have to complete a standard form of agreement.

This is not something to be too alarmed about, as the Revenue does provide a guidance to help complete the form. This is just the beginning, however, as each member then has to complete a return form 185. The two-part form must be completed for club members who leave during the year, as well as existing members.

Dates
It's crucial to complete any tax returns by due dates to avoid expensive penalties. Personal tax returns must be with the Revenue by January 31 in the year following the end of the financial year on April 5 to avoid an instant £100 fine. If you want the Revenue to work out your tax liability the deadline for completing self-assessment return is September 30 in the same year.

Help

The Inland Revenue should be able to explain what is required of your club, but the service has been particularly hard-pressed since the introduction of self-assessment a couple of years ago.

The Proshare Share Club Manual includes full details of taxation issues affecting clubs and, usefully, supplies copies of forms 185-1 and 185-2, which are all you need if your club qualifies for the simplified scheme.

CHAPTER TWELVE

AVOIDING THE TAXMAN

Like it or loathe it, if you make a bundle on the stock market, you're going to have to hand over a good proportion of the profits back to the taxman. We see it as a crime the government — and it doesn't matter what shade — commits on investors, since a fair old chunk of your profits go straight back to those duffers at the Treasury.

The buying and selling of shares is treated as a taxable activity. Any dividend payments are liable to income tax at the basic rate (23% for 1999/2000; 22% for 2000/2001) and the deduction is made at source. Higher-rate taxpayers must declare all dividends on their self-assessment tax form and pay accordingly.

But where the real injustice lies is that any profit made on the sale of shares is subject to capital gains tax (CGT). It's another means for the government to profit from your good fortune and looks as if it's designed to keep you poor in the process. Basically, if you dispose of an asset that is worth more that it was when you acquired it, you pay CGT on the difference.

In America the profits you make aren't subject to the same swingeing tax rules and it is no coincidence that a much higher proportion of the American population own shares. If British investors weren't taxed into oblivion the government would be able to encourage more people to own shares.

But every person in the UK (including children) has a CGT exemption of £7,200. ('Whoopee do! We'll all get rich on that,' we hear you say.) These sums are taxed at 20% for basic-rate taxpayers and 40% for higher-rate taxpayers. The tax-free allowance is calculated per person, so it is worth transferring shares to one's spouse, especially if he or she is a lower-rate taxpayer. Married couples can show a £14,400 profit before becoming liable to

CGT. Being unmarried (but both happily attached to delightful ladies) the Slickers have long thought that it's one of the few benefits of getting married. Neither of us have taken the plunge yet but soon we won't be able to afford to stay single since being a bachelor is becoming far too expensive!

Calculating CGT gains is a complicated process, which at its crudest amounts to the sale price minus the purchase price. However, there is an allowance to take account of inflation, which ended in April 1998. This allowance, called inflationary indexation protection, was designed to ensure that taxpayers were not taxed on profit that was little more than a reflection of rising prices. Any taxpayer who owns shares bought, say, five years ago is entitled to claim inflationary indexation protection for the five-year period up to April 1998, but not after that, because the allowance has ended. The precise calculation is a complicated one and some tax experts we know say even the Inland Revenue boys have difficulty with it.

Under self-assessment, the burden of estimating it has now shifted onto the ordinary taxpayer, who must now grapple with a terrifying calculation that would test even those annoying brats we knew at school who sat at the front and were brilliant at Maths.

Cutting down your tax bill

There are several ways of minimising the tax liability that is likely to arise from the sale of shares. An individual taxpayer who wants to sell shares at a price that will net a £14,400 profit can do so without incurring any CGT liability. First, he must sell the first tranche of shares at the end of one tax year — say March 30. A week later, now into the new tax year with a fresh £7,200 CGT allowance, he should sell the balance of his shares. The £14,400 profit will be free of CGT.

Married couples, obviously, fare twice as well and can net a £28,400 profit without incurring any CGT liability which, let's face it, is almost worth having. We must think about taking our girlfriends to the Silver Bells Wedding Chapel in Las Vegas where it takes about two minutes, and costs about $100, to get married!

What do you pay CGT on?

Any item can be judged as an asset for CGT purposes, but the most common assets include stocks and shares, land and buildings, and business assets, including goodwill. The biggest CGT exemption applies to the home you live in. However, if you have a second property, which you perhaps use as a holiday home, you'll be liable for CGT if you sell it for a profit.

If you had the foresight to squirrel away your shares in a Pep or an Isa (see the chapter on Isas for more information), then these are free of CGT — as is the interest from tax-exempt special savings accounts (Tessas) Other exemptions include private cars (most cars suffer from warp-drive depreciation rather than appreciation), National Savings Certificates, Premium Bonds and British Savings Bonds.

Can I avoid paying CGT?

The short answer is a simple 'No'. If you evade paying capital gains tax, you're breaking the law. Of course, when filling in your tax return, you may be tempted to be economical with the truth about how much of a capital gain you've made. If you made it in shares or property, you did all the work and took all the risk. Why share it with the taxman? Well, look at it like this: the Revenue estimates that it will investigate 5% of the 10 million tax returns it gets each year. These people have seen every dodge in the book, so it's unlikely yours will fool them for very long.

However, the taxman does cut you a break in the

shape of something called tapering relief. Like CGT itself, tapering relief is simple in theory, but hellishly complicated in practice. Tapering relief means the longer you have held an asset, the less tax is payable on it. It encourages people to hold their assets for longer, rather than cut and run for a quick profit. For more in-depth information on how tapering relief works, check out the relevant pages from the Inland Revenue guide. Remember that business assets are subject to one set of tax rates and non-business assets another, so don't confuse the two.

The only other way to reduce your CGT bill is if you have incurred losses, which are offset against gains. The trick is to do it in the same or subsequent tax year. You can't carry a loss back, meaning you can't sell something at a loss in this tax year and hope to apply it to last year's tax return. However, you can carry a loss forward, so a loss incurred in the last tax year can be included in this year's return.

What do I do now?
Capital gains tax is one of those areas that becomes more complicated the more you look into it. A tax partner with one of the 'big five' global accountancy firms said recently that in recent years, the CGT system has become so complex as to defy

simplification. To compute your CGT liabilities you have to know how tapering relief works and is applied. Or else you could end up giving more to the taxman than you need to.

If you're one of those looking at a capital gain way above your annual allowance, you might consider spending some of that gain on a tax accountant. If you think you will have a big CGT bill, an accountant could save you a considerable amount of money.

Enterprise Investment Schemes

Tax exposure can be minimised still further by reinvesting the proceeds from the sale of shares. This can be done through the Enterprise Investment Scheme (EIS) or through a Venture Capital Trust (VCT), but this is where things can get complicated.

The idea of the EIS is that people who have made a substantial profit on the sale of shares should be encouraged to find another savings home for their money. The EIS works by allowing taxpayers to invest in the unquoted shares of a proper trading company. They can thus roll their gain into the reinvestment. Professional advisers are useful here, since they can put prospective investors in touch with directors of these unquoted companies and advise on their suitability for investment.

The traditional exit route is flotation — the unquoted company comes to the stock market, lists and then gives its backers the opportunity to sell their shares. As per usual any profit made at this stage will still be liable to tax, but the liability arising from the profit on the first sale of shares was wiped out when the money was reinvested in the unquoted company.

VCTs work in a similar way to investment trusts. A sponsor (usually a venture capitalist) puts together a portfolio of investments — called a trust. These investments usually consist of start-up and fledgling companies at an early stage of development that have satisfied all the usual, stringent venture capital criteria. Backers, such as investors who have made profits from the sale of their previous share portfolios, put money into that trust and the money is spread among a range of EIS-type companies. Tax is only incurred when any profit on that investment is subsequently realised. Investors should be aware, however, that a VCT does not carry any guarantees of performance and that they may not get back the money they have invested.

Income tax

Dividends are paid net of tax at the basic rate, so

higher-rate taxpayers have an extra liability to pay after receiving their dividend pay-outs. The difference between the 23% paid at source and the 40% liability works out at 25% of the total received in dividends.

There is no way of avoiding the income tax liability, but there are ways of minimising its impact — for instance by allowing a spouse who is a low- or basic-rate taxpayer to hold shares instead, and thereby avoid the higher-rate liability.

Alternatively, taxpayers who don't want to pay a lot of tax on their shareholdings might want to consider investing in shares that do not pay out large sums in dividends. By opting for capital growth instead, they can watch their shares appreciate in value and only pay tax on any profit made when they are sold.

Using the capital gains tax allowances outlined above, tax exposure can be minimised or even eliminated. Some investors may wish to invest in zero-coupon preference shares, which pay no dividend whatsoever. These shares are bought in the market at a pre-determined rate. Shareholders have the advantage of knowing for certain what level they will be redeemed at in future. There is no income tax liability because there is no share dividend pay-out, but any growth in the value of the preference share will be treated as a capital gain.

Another advantage is that the taxpayer has the advantage of being able to plan ahead for tax purposes, knowing exactly what the CGT liability — if any — will be. Preference shares are a low-risk way of investing in companies, albeit at a lower potential return than might be obtained from buying ordinary shares, and well worth considering for any investor who would rather have a capital gain than dividends.

Stamp duty

Once again, this is a government-backed con trick that only exists because it has been around so long that nobody can be bothered to abolish it. Any government who planned to axe the damn thing would get our vote — and if they took a machete to CGT too they would probably be in power for 100 years!

Stamp duty is one of the oldest forms of tax, but today it only applies to three main areas: the transfer of some business assets, buying and selling stocks and shares, and buying property or leases. Investors pay stamp duty each time they buy shares. The tax is charged at a flat rate of 0.5% of the deal. On property, stamp duty is in bands. Homes over

£60,000 but under £250,000 attract stamp duty at 1%. Between £250,000 and £500,000 the tax is 3%. Over £500,000 it is 4%. There is no stamp duty on properties costing less than £60,000.

One of the disadvantages of having a tax system that has developed over time is that it can be a mishmash that only a handful of experts understand. Nowhere is this more so than in the case of stamp duty. We reckon it is a 300-year old duty long past its sell-by date. It is levied at 0.5% on the value of shares bought. So if someone buys £100,000 of shares, it will cost £500 to register their ownership. It is not a huge burden but it is nevertheless an irritant that can make inroads into your profits.

There had been much speculation that stamp duty's time was up at the last Budget. In the end, however, the Chancellor left it alone. This has prompted some tax experts to conclude that something will definitely be done soon. Currently the government shows no signs of wanting to change its stance. If only the losers would realise what a vote-winner it would be to make the necessary changes to the tax system.

Stamp duty raises £5.7 billion for the nation's coffers every year, equivalent to 6p in the pound of income tax. This compares with £2 billion a year raised from inheritance tax — another tax that should have its head on the block — and £3.2 billion from capital gains tax.

Many tax accountants wish the government, if it plans to continue with stamp duty, would at least modernise the system and update legislation that was mostly drafted in the late nineteenth century — and some of which came into being over 300 years ago.

Tax avoidance

We Slickers are greatly in favour of tax avoidance, which is why we shell out good money every year for an accountant who, for a few hundred quid, can save us thousands. We're not advocating breaking the law — that would be as foolish as Britain's antiquated tax law itself — but remember to get the guy who knows all the tricks of his trade. He will invariably be the one wearing the widest pinstripes! The wider the better. Unfortunately, the Labour government has taken a hard line on tax avoidance, seeming at times to lump it together with tax evasion, which is illegal. This is an important distinction, so let's spell it out again: tax evasion is illegal but tax avoidance is absolutely fine.

There is nothing wrong with avoiding tax. Just

stay within the rules. Look upon tax avoidance as a perk — after all, the government tries to screw investors with its CGT, so why shouldn't you operate within the law to see that you get as much of it back as possible, or don't pay it in the first place? Taxpayers are not obliged to pay more tax than they should under law. The tax system has a number of allowances and incentives that make it possible to pay less tax, especially on investments.

The first step is to make sure you are claiming any allowances you are entitled to and, if you are covered by Pay As You Earn (PAYE), that you have the right tax coding. The Revenue will help check these points. Investing in tax-efficient ways, for example through an Isa, is not only perfectly legal but encouraged by the government. There are ways to reduce exposure to capital gains tax and inheritance tax, but planning requires professional advice.

As part of the self-assessment system, introduced for the 1997–1998 tax year, the Inland Revenue has taken a more proactive interest in taxpayers' affairs. In 1997–1998, there were 16,110 full enquiries into self-assessment returns from business taxpayers, and 22,000 investigations into non-business items on returns. By 1998–1999 these numbers had soared. In that year there were 43,713 enquiries into business taxpayers, and 248,000 enquiries into non-business items on returns. Yes, that's a quarter of a million — which the Inland Revenue would like us all to believe is an insignificant proportion of the total taxpayer population (some nine million self-assessment tax forms were issued that year).

The message is clear: the Revenue boys are now ten times more likely to have a good look at your return so be extremely careful when filling it in.

Tax advice

Although the self-assessment tax form is designed to be as easy to understand as any such document could be, some taxpayers may feel that they need professional advice. Although help with filling in the form itself can be obtained from the Inland Revenue, for comprehensive advice and tax planning guidance, a qualified tax expert should be consulted.

The Chartered Institute of Taxation can provide details of tax advisers in your area, as can the Institute of Chartered Accountants in England & Wales or the Institute of Chartered Accountants in Scotland.

Self-assessment

Most people pay their tax through Pay As You Earn

(PAYE), which means the boss takes the taxman's share out of your monthly pay packet. For people with reasonably basic financial arrangements, that's all there is to it.

But for millions of others, tax is not that simple. They have to deal with self-assessment. This is the system for collecting extra tax from investments, savings, renting property and self-employment. Under these rules, it's you, not the taxman, who does the hard work.

What is self-assessment?

Simply, it's the system for paying tax on money that's not taxed at source, or not taxed enough. About nine million people are covered by the system.

Under self-assessment, taxpayers declare their own income and — optionally — work out the tax due. For people with fairly simple circumstances, such as some dividend income, it's not too daunting. For taxpayers with more complicated affairs or the self-employed, it can be a time-consuming task and it might pay to use a tax adviser or accountant.

What does it apply to?

Any earnings that are taxed under PAYE are not covered by self-assessment. Nor are income and dividend payments where tax is deducted at source, unless you are a higher-rate taxpayer.

Earnings that are not taxed come under self-assessment. The self-employed, who are usually paid gross, have to pay their tax under the system. So do people who have casual untaxed earnings, earnings from property, or income on overseas dividends or savings. Higher-rate taxpayers use self-assessment to pay the difference between the tax they are due to pay and the tax deducted by the investment company or savings bank. Company directors and trustees also need to fill in self-assessment forms.

It's the taxpayer's responsibility to follow the self-assessment rules. Not having a form is no excuse. If you think you fall under the self-assessment regime, ask the Inland Revenue for a form.

What about these deadlines we keep hearing about?

Self-assessment has rigid deadlines with fines and penalties for taxpayers who fail to comply. Forms are normally sent in April. Taxpayers who want the Revenue to work out the tax bill — there is no charge for this — have until September 30 to return their forms. If your tax bill is less than £1,000 and you want the tax you owe included in your tax code for the next year, you must also return the form by the end of September.

If you work out your own tax, the deadline is January 31 after the end of the tax year. This is also the deadline for paying any tax you owe. The taxman might also ask you to make payments on account (in advance) twice a year: this applies to almost all the self-employed, and those with large unearned incomes.

Payments on account usually total half the tax the Inland Revenue expects you to pay in the next/current financial year. The deadlines are January 31 in the tax year and July 31 immediately after it. However, it's hard for taxpayers and the Revenue to make precise predictions of what your tax bill will be, so you may have to make a balancing payment the next January. Penalties for late returns are stiff: there's a £100 fine for late returns, and the Revenue can, and almost always will, charge interest on tax that's paid late.

Help!
The simplest place to turn for help is the documentation that comes with the tax return itself. Work through the form methodically and it shouldn't be that difficult. One point to remember is keeping

good records during the year will save time when you come to fill in your form.

The self-employed should already be keeping accurate books and records, but it will help to make sure that information, such as expenses, is recorded in a similar way to the way the Revenue wants it.

The Inland Revenue offers a range of help options. Taxpayers can call at a local tax centre, or ring the Self Assessment helpline (0645 000 444). Alternatively, the Revenue's website has all the help files and copies of the forms.

Software such as Intuit's Quicken, Microsoft Tax Saver and Which? TaxCalc can all help work out self-assessment returns. They're widely available. If you want advice, the Chartered Institute of Taxation can put you in touch with a qualified tax adviser.

Inheritance tax

How are you going to beat the grim reaper is a question you should start considering as early as possible. Inheritance tax (IHT) is known as a tax on the rich. Yet this couldn't be further than the truth. An increasing number of ordinary families are falling within the inheritance tax bracket — the result of booming share prices and rising house values. Yet it is quite simple to reduce an inheritance tax bill with careful tax planning.

How much?

Inheritance tax affects any estate worth more than £234,000. That covers all your assets — your house, its contents, investments, other assets and perhaps money accumulated in a pension fund. Once the threshold is reached, IHT is charged at a swingeing rate of 40%. With the average house now worth close to £80,000 nationally and almost twice that in much of the South, it's easy to see how IHT is an issue for more and more people.

Use your allowance

The first thing to do is just think ahead and use your allowance properly. There's no IHT to pay on money left to a spouse so if you leave everything to them, you will have wasted your allowance and could be putting a higher tax burden on your children and grandchildren.

If, for example, you have left assets of £500,000 to your spouse, he or she will not have to pay any tax. When your spouse dies (assuming the capital remained intact), your children would not have to pay tax on the first £234,000 but would face a bill of £106,400 on the remaining £266,000. You could reduce your IHT liability by bequeathing £234,000 directly to your children and leaving the remaining £266,000 to your spouse. Neither would pay IHT when you die, as before. The real difference comes when your spouse dies. At that point, the money bequeathed to your spouse (£266,000) would be passed onto the children. They would get the £234,000 allowance, leaving £32,000 subject to IHT. That would leave the children with a bill of £12,800 — £93,600 less than if all the money had been left to your spouse.

Give it away

You can also give money away. Gifts made during the donor's lifetime (known, as lifetime gifts) don't usually count for IHT. This is known under the tax rules as a Potentially Exempt Transfer, or PET. As long as the gift is made outright to an individual or to certain types of trust, there will be no further tax to pay. The gift does need to be genuine. The Inland Revenue will not allow gifts where the giver keeps an interest in the asset. For example, if you gave your house to your children but still lived in it, the Revenue is likely to disallow the gift.

Special rules apply for seven years before the donor's death, which is why a PET is only potentially exempt. Gifts made during the last seven years of the donor's life attract tapered relief from inheritance tax.

There is no relief if you die within three years, but live for four years and the relief is 20%, for five it's 40%, six it's 60% and in the seventh year, 80%. In addition, each individual can give away £3,000 a year without it being subject to any tax at all. Small gifts, of £250 or less, are also exempt from IHT.

Where there's a will

There are ways to limit inheritance tax bills, especially through the use of trusts. But one of the most straightforward measures everyone should take is to make a will. Without a will, inheritance tax bills can be much higher than need be.

Dying without a will is known as dying 'intestate'. There are fixed rules governing how money is passed on. However, different rules on intestacy apply under the law in Scotland and Northern Ireland and the law in England and Wales.

In the case of England and Wales, if you are married and there are children, the surviving spouse inherits personal effects, the next £125,000, and the income for half the remainder of the estate for life. The rest is subject to IHT. If there is a will and the husband leaves it all to the wife, or vice versa, there is no tax to pay. As the cost of a will starts at less than £100, this is a valuable investment.

However, differing scenarios apply in each jurisdiction where circumstances differ, for instance, if the couple weren't married. The complexity of this matter highlights the need to plan ahead to ensure you don't leave a legal minefield for those you care for, plus the possibility of a very unwelcome tax bill.

Let insurance take the strain
One further option to consider is a life assurance policy, set up to pay an IHT bill. An independent financial adviser or a solicitor will be able to organise this. The insurance should be 'written in trust', so the payment goes to the surviving relatives — and therefore to those who have to pay the tax bill.

CHAPTER THIRTEEN

ISAS

We've already seen how the taxman likes to rob investors of a significant proportion of their profits by levying some very unfair taxes. Well, the good news is that investors have a chance to get some of it back.

It's not often that the taxman lets us pay less tax. Almost every time we earn or spend money, the taxman takes his cut. But if you are saving money, there are legal ways to protect it from the grasp of the Revenue boys — by sheltering your investments under an Individual Savings Account (Isa). Put simply, an Isa is a tax-fee umbrella that enables you to legally shelter cash, equities and insurance from income tax and capital gains tax. OK, you're not going to become a millionaire from what you have in your Isa but it is a nice 'leg-up' from the government and it would be churlish to ignore it.

The scheme was introduced by the government in April 1999 to replace Peps and Tessas and is designed to encourage us to save more. We are great fans of any tax-free scheme that the government introduces and strongly recommend that investors use their allowance to protect a section of their savings from taxes.

For a government-backed freebie Isas got a bit of a lukewarm reception, largely because they are more difficult to understand than Peps and Tessas and have smaller tax breaks. Investors could save up to £9,000 a year in Peps and a further £9,000 over five years in Tessas. That's more than double the Isa allowance. But the tax shelter is still well worth having, providing you invest for the long term — so start one up now.

What types of Isa are available?

There are three types of Isa — cash, equity and insurance Isas. A cash Isa can either be a simple deposit account or a cash unit trust. The equity Isa covers a whole host of stock-market investments, including unit trusts, shares and investment trusts. An insurance Isa is a shelter for investment bonds issued by insurance companies, such as with-profit bonds. These bonds invest in the stock market and include an element of life assurance.

Not all companies will offer every option — many fund managers, for example, will only offer equity Isas — and deciding which combination is best for you will depend on the type of investor you are — your approach to risk and how long you plan to save.

How much can you invest?

To get Isas off the ground, the government has extended the £7,000 allowance it gave investors in 1999/2000 to the current tax year. If you invested before April 5, 2000, you will have been able to put up to £7,000 into an Isa. You could either have put the entire amount in an equity Isa (shares) or split your allowance between the three types, with a maximum of £3,000 going into cash and £1,000 into insurance. The rest could have been put into equities.

Tax allowances work on a 'use it or lose it' basis — if you didn't invest by April 5, 2000, the £7,000 allowance will have been lost forever. If you didn't use it, don't despair — there is always this year, although the annual allowance has dropped to £5,000 (£10,000 for a married couple). Again, you can put all this into equities, or place £1,000 in cash, £1,000 in insurance and £3,000 in equities.

Should you buy a mini or maxi Isa?

If you choose a maxi Isa, your full allowance must be invested with a single company. If you prefer to use different firms, perhaps a unit trust company for your equity Isa and a building society for your cash Isa, you have to take out separate mini Isas. But this option carries a sting in the tail — it cuts the amount you can invest in equities from £7,000 to just £3,000. Your choice is crucial as you cannot take out a mini and maxi Isa in the same tax year. But most experts agree that if you are saving long term, it makes sense to put as much as you can into equities as the returns you can expect are far higher. We reckon this makes the maxi Isa a clear winner for long-term investors.

Can you switch Isas?

This is where the rules baffle everyone — even the experts. You can swap from one Isa manager to another, even in the same tax year, providing you stick with the same type of Isa. So, you could switch from a mini Isa to a mini Isa, but not from a mini to a maxi.

The government also prevents you from switching between the cash, equity and insurance elements of the Isa. You cannot, for example, switch from a cash to an equity Isa, so take care to make the right choice from the start.

Can you take out your money?

Yes. But remember that the Isa is designed to encourage long-term saving. If you take money out of an equity Isa within five years and stock markets have not performed well, you might get back less than you invested.

In addition, any money you take out of your Isa will still count towards your Isa allowance. If, for example, you invested £7,000 in the last tax year and took out £3,000 after a few months, you cannot put back the £3,000 at a later date.

What is a Cat-standard?

This is an official stamp of approval for Isas which meet certain minimum standards on cost, access and terms (Cat). The standards are voluntary and aim to ensure investors get a fair deal but there is no guarantee that these Isas will perform better.

What happens to your Pep and Tessa?

You have not been able to take out new Peps or Tessas since April 6, 1999, but any money you have invested in these schemes remains ring-fenced from the taxman. You cannot pay any extra cash into your existing Peps but can switch to a different fund company if you are not happy with your fund's performance.

Tessas are different — you can continue contributing to your existing Tessa until it matures. You then have six months to switch the original capital (but not the interest) into a cash Isa, in addition to your usual Isa allowance.

Many companies have launched special cash Isas for people who have maturing Tessas.

What to put in your Isa

One of the great advantages that an Isa has over the Pep is that a wider choice of investments can be sheltered from tax. It's important to bear in mind that an Isa isn't an investment in itself, but simply the name of the wrapper you can put around an investment to avoid paying tax on gains and dividends. To help you make an informed choice, here are the main investments that can be put in an Isa, and their pros and cons.

Unit trusts

These have traditionally been UK investors' favourite way to spread the risk of investing in the stock market. They work by pooling the money from thousands of investors, thereby spreading the risk by buying a wider range of stocks than people could afford to buy directly. There are more than 1,000 unit trusts and open-ended investment companies (Oeics) — an updated, more flexible version of a unit trust — which means there's plenty of choice of funds.

Unit trust companies do, however, charge a management fee for their services, as well as making money on the bid to offer spread between selling and buying units. This means that they can work out quite expensive. You can normally expect to pay an upfront fee of around 5% and an annual management fee of 1%, although managers usually offer a discount of around 2% on the upfront charge if you buy the fund in an Isa. You can also cut your costs by buying through a discount broker.

Investment trusts

These have been the focus of a multi-million-pound marketing push in recent times to improve their profile. They are similar to unit trusts in that they are also pooled investments, but investment trusts are actually set up as companies and have their shares quoted on the stock market. There are a huge range of trusts which invest in a range of UK and overseas stock markets.

Because investment trusts are actually quoted shares, their price can rise or fall with market sentiment and may have little relation to the actual worth of the fund.

Offshore funds

You are allowed to put offshore funds in an Isa. These have been attractive in the past as they allow you to delay paying tax on your investments, but you may as well buy onshore funds as all gains within an Isa are tax-free in any case.

Bonds and gilts

These are fixed interest investments that are designed to provide you with an income. Bonds and derivatives are issued by companies and gilts by the government and are generally regarded to be a safer investment than straight shares. However, they give little growth and are only for those seeking a fixed income.

Company shares

Buying the shares of a company directly through an Isa can mean making major savings if your portfolio rises as much as you hope it will. For example, if you bought £7,000 worth of shares and they doubled, you would be in danger of passing the capital gains tax threshold of £7,200. Put the shares within an Isa and there are no tax liabilities and therefore no worries.

Share options

These work by giving you the option to buy shares in your company at a set price in the future. If you exercise your option to buy the shares then you have 90 days to transfer them into an Isa. This can help reduce any capital gains tax liability that may have built up. However you may only be able to transfer part of your share options if they have risen by a lot as you must keep to the annual £7,000 limit in an Isa.

DIY Isas

It's generally well known that DIY can save you

money. Rather than pay a builder or a decorator, you just pay for the materials and do the donkey work yourself. The same goes for investments. Ask a financial adviser or a stockbroker for investment advice, and it'll cost you. Pick the stocks yourself and, after paying the stamp duty and broker's fee, you won't have to stump up for management charges. And, if you wrap the stocks in a self-select Isa, you won't be stung for capital gains tax either. The big mistake any investor could make is thinking that a self-select Isa is simply a tax dodge by any other name.

Yes, those shares in that Internet IPO you bagged on issue have grown by 30,000% and no, Gordon Brown doesn't want a slice of your profits because the shares are wrapped up in that Isa. However, a self-select Isa is not a wonderful device to squirrel away shares you already own and thereby sidestep the grasping paw of the Inland Revenue.

Take Durlacher. You bought the shares in late November last year and they cost you 710p each. By early March, these shares were trading at £34.02, a rise of 379%. If you invested £5,000 then, three months later, your investment is worth £23,950. Take away your initial investment and your capital gains tax allowance of £7,100 and you're left with a capital gain of £11,850. Not bad. Unfortunately, if you sell the shares, the Inland Revenue will want 40% of that gain, a cool £4,740. No problem, you think. I'll simply stick the shares in a self-select Isa and save myself a fortune. Er, sorry — that ain't allowed.

It's a popular misconception to think that a self-select Isa is some magic bag into which you can transfer assets and avoid capital gains tax. You can't give your self-select Isa manager shares. You can only give them cash on account and instruct them which shares to buy on your behalf. So, if you already own the shares it's too late. The only exception to this strictly observed rule is company share option schemes. If you exercise options to buy shares in the company you work for, you have 90 days from the exercise date in which to shelter the shares in a self-select Isa. But this is the only exception.

But back to those Durlacher shares. If you want to shelter them from CGT in an Isa, you would first have to sell them and then instruct your Isa manager to buy them back with the money you have raised. The good news is that you don't have to wait the obligatory 30 days between selling and buying back, so you should be able to buy them back at roughly the price that you sold at.

The bad news is that you have to pay stamp duty,

broker's fees and, if you incur it, CGT. You can't escape your CGT responsibilities. If you sell the shares and the gain realised is less than your annual allowance of £7,200, then there's no CGT to pay. But if they are worth more, you can sell them and buy them back within an Isa. You will have to pay CGT when you first sell them but once they are in the Isa, your cash is safe.

Is it worth your while? It all depends if you think the shares are about to rocket in value. Selling them, paying the CGT, then buying them back and paying stamp duty could be an expensive business. But it could be worth it in the long run.

Say you invest the maximum £7,000 (£5,000 for 2000/2001). If, over the course of time, this investment doubles in value to £14,000, it does so free of CGT liability. This is where a self-select Isa can come into its own. You can instruct your Isa manager to sell half your holding and reinvest the realised cash into other shares. As long as the Isa manager is not paying you the proceeds in cash and that money stays within the Isa envelope, then it's not liable for CGT.

You can change your shares within the Isa as many times as the manager will allow, although if you withdraw cash from the Isa, you can't then reinvest it at a later date. However, you do have the freedom to change the shares in self-select Isas taken out in tax years other than the current one. The contents of the Isa isn't locked when the tax year changes.

Where can you get them?

All that said, If you still fancy yourself as a stock picker and want a self-select Isa, where do you go? Self-selects are available from a number of providers, such as Barclays, NatWest and Halifax. But to really cut costs to the bone, the cheapest way to go is on line.

Some great deals are offered by execution-only brokers such as Charles Schwab. The dealing charges usually range from a minimum of £15 a deal to a maximum of £50. And you still have to pay 0.5% stamp duty on any shares they purchase on your behalf. On top of a dealing fee and the dreaded stamp duty, self-select Isa managers also levy a quarterly administration fee. In the case of Schwab, it charges 0.1875% a quarter on the value of your portfolio with a minimum charge of £5.

The greater the value of your holding, the more in management fees you save if you DIY. So going down the DIY route could not only save you a bundle in fees, but could also tap you into those raging growth stocks that can quadruple in value overnight.

However, there Is an argument that DIY just means selling building and decorating materials at rock-bottom prices to the technically inept. Anybody can buy a sack of plaster and mix it with water. Applying it evenly to the wall or ceiling takes skill and could mean calling in a proper builder to rectify your mistakes. So if you feel you're one of these types of investors, you may be better off sticking with a managed Isa. It'll cost, but not nearly as much as picking a duff share would. Losses are losses, after all.

CHAPTER FOURTEEN
TWELVE-MONTH GUIDE TO A MILLION

Congratulations. Having got this far, not only should you know how to make a good punt on the market and how to avoid giving all your profits to the taxman, but you probably know more than most of the so-called experts out there. Ready to roll? Well, how long you spend learning and how much you spend investing is entirely up to you. But the Slickers have put together a twelve-month plan, to help you pace yourself on a journey through the stock market.

Month One

At this stage, assume you know absolutely nothing about shares. So it's time to learn. Forget about buying anything, forget about even ever making any cash.

The first step is to familiarise yourself with the basics. We would kick off by getting just one quality newspaper every day, without fail. Our own preference is the *Independent*, the business section of which is the most readable. Don't feel you have to know every deal going on out there, but try to get a feel for what's happening. Simple things: is the market crashing or booming? You'll be amazed how many people don't know this when they start investing.

Try to get a picture of what's happening in the economy as a whole. Which sectors are booming, and which are in trouble? And most important of all, get a feel for some of the smaller companies out there. The smaller stories in the paper are usually the more interesting ones. After all, these are the companies where you are likely to make most of your cash.

Learning should be fun and can take time. Just 15 minutes every morning for a whole month, and you'll be amazed how much more you know about the City.

You could spend money on specialist publications like the *Investors Chronicle* and *The Economist*. Personally, apart from the pose value, we think they are a waste of time. Stick to the paper, and take it slowly.

Month Two

Now you should have a general understanding of what's happening in the business world, so it's time to delve a little deeper. Again, at this stage we still don't recommend making any investment decisions for real. All you've done is spend 15 minutes a day reading the business pages. So be patient.

The next step is to start monitoring share prices and related news stories. Our favourite, and the cheapest, method of doing this, is to use the Internet. The best website is iii.co.uk, which gives you a daily round-up of the biggest winners and losers of the day — a listing of the biggest changes (by percentage) in share prices on the day at any given moment.

Make it your business to check this information at least once a day. And having checked the prices, look behind the reasons. You should find that on the website too. By now, you are starting to get a feel for specific companies. You should start noticing patterns — for example, how one company has seen its share price more than double in the space of a week, while others have constantly fallen.

You should also start coming across companies you never knew existed, until you saw them on the top ten list. Find out a bit more about them — what do they do? Are all companies in that sector doing the same?

Month Three

By this stage, you should have a pretty good feel for the market, and precisely where some of the action is. It's time to get ready for your first deal. We haven't suggested you get a broker until now, because the moment you do you are bound to want to start trading.

So get one! As we said, the smaller the better. If you are lucky, you could set up the account on the phone. The odds are it will take a week. Never mind — use that week to find out more about the City.

And so, finally, the moment has arrived. Time to spend some cash. We suggest your first deal isn't spectacular. In fact, it should be as boring as possible. What has been the safest company around lately? Make sure it's in the FTSE-100, and that its price isn't moving much.

Ring up the broker and place an order for £500 of shares in the company on a T+10 basis. And remember, sell the damn shares before the time is up. You might make a few quid at the very least, or lose a few. Doesn't matter. Now you know how to deal with a broker, how to buy shares, and how to sell shares.

Month Four

Having got the hang of buying and selling shares, you now need to focus on actually making some money. There's nothing like choosing a big winner when you kick off, and you might as well try straight away. For the whole of this first week, monitor the top ten winners and losers list on a website. This should give you a good indication of what's happening to specific companies during that period of time.

Look out for a big company that has seen its shares drop by more than 10% for reasons outside its control: such as a fall in the US market or concerns about the economy in the UK. Whatever. Just look out for reasons that have nothing directly to do with the company.

You should be able to find a technology stock here. Having found one that has seen a considerable amount of its stock market value wiped out during one day alone, give your broker a ring at about 4.15pm and buy £1,000 worth on a T+10 account. It's important to book the shares around this time. Any earlier and the shares will still be tumbling. However, in the last few minutes of trading many shares stage a late recovery, so you want to get in before the price starts going back up again.

Done it? Now sit back and pray! This is your first

real gamble, but if you've called it right, you should see the price start rising again the following day. Hopefully by as much as it fell the previous day, if not more. But make sure you sell before the end of the day. You should have made over £100 if everything went according to plan.

The losers list is a good way to kick off your share dealing. It helps you find out about companies in more detail, and you can bank a good return if you play it right.

We suggest you keep this up for a month. There's no pressure to make a trade every week. Just go with what you feel comfortable with, and whatever you do don't risk more than a grand or it could go horribly wrong.

Month Five

From losers, move on to winners. Unlike last month, you'll have to get out of bed earlier this time. Your target is a company that has benefited from positive news, and has a share price that is rising steadily — but not spectacularly. Often, these are smaller companies that the City is still mulling over. Your goal is to get in before most investors, including the financial institutions, who make their daily decisions after 11am. You are searching for a company where the share price has risen between 4% to 8% by 8.30am. That should be your strike time.

Again, with a £1,000 punt on a T+10 account, you could end up with a gain of 12% or more on the day. But remember to sell before the market closes, around 4.20pm. Other sellers, including institutions, get involved at this time and can send the price lower. If you've played the market right, you could be sitting on at least £100 clear profit per trade.

Keep at this. Start to get to know the companies you are dealing with a bit better, as many will often reappear on the list.

Over the next few weeks, become more focussed on this strategy, and mix it with the technique of picking companies on the losers list. If things are going well, you can gradually start increasing the amount of money you are investing, although we suggest you don't go above £5,000.

Also, remember to keep selling — otherwise you will end up with over £20,000 invested in the market and no way of paying for the shares. At all times, you don't want to be hanging on to the shares for over a day.

Month Six
By now you have had a reasonable dabble in the

market and should have a good idea of what is happening in the City. You should be in a better position to start spotting winning companies. And you are looking for serious winners from now.

It is time to start broadening your horizons, and taking an interest in specific sectors. Keep playing the winners and losers game (unless it's going disastrously wrong), but start searching for those growth stocks we talked about. Think about where the action is at this time of the year: are biotech companies doing well? Is media the craze? Is the Internet going mad again? Or are we all obsessed with new vacuum cleaners?

Wherever the action is, your job is to get in before the rest of the pack. Use your common sense, nothing more, to judge which company in a booming sector is about to take off. And remember, it's usually a company not directly involved in that sector but a spin-off firm. As the month progresses, increase your investments in these, looking to have shares in at least four different growth stocks.

Month Seven

Your share dealing has by now become more active and, we hope, very fruitful. It's time to make it more planned: monitor carefully what you are doing, and ensure that you haven't got more than 20 investments out at any one time. How widely are your investments made? If they are all in technology, you'd better change things quickly. This is the month in which you really start to build up your portfolio. Ensure you have shares in the growing sectors of the time, take a few in safe sectors for longer-term positions, and structure your short-term punts: if you feel you have perfected the art of short-term investments, look for about two a week with up to £10,000 invested on a T+10 account. On at least one, you should look for a 40% return on the investment. At the same time, some of the stocks you picked earlier should be showing steady progress. If they are, and the market view is that things will only get better, steadily increase the amount you have invested in those companies.

Month Eight

This is the time to start liquidating some of your stocks. You should be well up on quite a few, but be realistic. If a share has risen 300% in price since you first bought it, will it get much better? Are you not just being greedy? The key to success is not when you buy, but when you sell. Take out the cash from some profitable shares. Of the money you get back, DON'T reinvest it all. In fact, only put back a little bit into the market, preferably on some highly speculative shares that could get you a decent return.

Month Nine

If things are looking settled, you should now start searching for the really big hit that will make you an absolute fortune: a share suspension. We recommend that by this stage, if you are making a decent income from shares, think about getting a Reuters terminal. This is the best system on which to spot the action quickly.

Most of all, you are looking for a small company that most people have never heard of, which is suddenly filling up its boardroom with some big names. Why are they all joining this tin-pot firm? Something must be happening.

If you feel sure, then get ready for the biggest gamble of your life. Put £5,000 or more into it — assuming you can by now afford to pay for the shares. If you have picked a winner, the shares are likely to be suspended for several weeks before they re-list, meaning you will have to pay up for them.

But it should be worth it. A good share suspension could bring you back up to 1,000% straight profit.

Month Ten

If you're on a winning streak, then gradually increase

your trading in the 'winners and losers list'. Having stuck a grand a time before, you should feel comfortable placing orders for between £5,000 and £10,000 on shares you suspect will rise sharply the next day. This could bring you over £1,000 in profit each time. Also, go for more expert techniques, such as spotting trading volumes. With a good idea of what's going on in the City, you should be able to spot the deals before they happen. With a Reuters screen, you should be able to spot a forthcoming company announcement — this is the time to move in for the kill, before the rest of the pack.

Month Eleven

Take a good look at your portfolio and start making some serious decisions. In particular, think about getting rid of shares where not much has happened. Even if you have lost a bit of money on them, it doesn't matter. Cut and run while you are still ahead of the rest. Focus more on the growth stocks again, looking out for a big punt on fast-moving sectors. We suggest biotechs: at least once a month a company in this sector makes an announcement on some new drug that will change our lives forever. It never does, but pick the right company and it could change your finances forever.

And what about that share suspension? Has it come through? If so, you could be sitting on a very large amount of cash.

Month Twelve

Add up the value of every single share you have, and how much profit you are sitting on. Having played the market right, this could be a huge amount of dosh — hopefully £1 million.

If it is, and we hope it is, we have some very simple advice for you. Sell all your shares, take the cash and enjoy the rest of your life — and never more play the stock market. It will never get this good again.

JARGON BUSTER

This is the Slickers' essential guide to all the confusing lingo that you're likely to hear if you venture into the world of stocks and shares. These phrases are generally spoken loudly into a mobile phone whilst walking into a cappuccino bar in the City. The Slickers recommend that you don't do that, as it will make you look like a bit of a wally.

What we do recommend that you do is have a quick glance through them so that you've got a vague idea of what people are on about — and if you know your CGT from your EPS, you're more likely to

trouser a packet! Learn five of them a day, and you'll
soon know more than the so-called experts...

Actively-Managed: Term used to describe the investment strategy of a fund which has its portfolio actively invested by its manager. The manager is supposed to seek out what he or she considers good or promising stocks and shares and invests part of the fund in them in an effort to produce above average returns, although the bozos often get it wrong.

American Depository Receipt (ADR): A UK share that can be bought or sold on the US Stock Exchange. British Telecom is listed on the UK Stock Exchange, but the company's ADRs trade on the US Stock Exchange.

Advisory Stockbroker: Stockbrokers who offer advice on which shares to buy and sell. But in this day and age it's better to do it yourself — why give a broker all your cash and let him have all the fun?

Alternative Investment Market (AIM): Regulated by the London Stock Exchange, this market is designed for small, young and growing companies. They're higher risk than those on the 'Official List' — but a helluva lot more fun.

Analyst: A City professional who analyses companies all day to work out their value. The term is generally applied to any professional investor who does research of some kind. Why not call yourself an analyst next time your down the boozer with your mates?

Annual Report: A yearly statement of a public company's operating and financial performance that includes pretty pictures of the board. However, there are so many accounting rules a company can use to put a gloss on its results that we take a lot of what we read in these with a pinch of salt.

Asset: An asset is anything that benefits its owner. In investment, assets can be tangible, such as stock and shares, cash or property, or intangible such as copyrights, trademarks, brand names and other invisible bits of property.

Asset Stripping: When a company is acquired, the new owner often 'asset strips' by flogging off its patents, successful offshoots, property and other assets to make a profit on the deal. Sometimes, businesses are retained and turned into profitable enterprises with the help of new management. The best asset strippers are all called James — Goldsmith, Hanson, Slater and Mellon — so there is hope for Slicker Hipwell yet.

Balance of Trade: The difference between the value of a country's imports and exports of saleable goods. The figure excludes money from tourism, insurance and banking.

Balance Sheet: A statement produced at regular intervals, normally at the end of a firm's financial year. It shows a breakdown of what the company owns, how much money is in the bank and how much money it owes. It is often found in the company's annual report but as we've said you can take a lot of what a company says with a large dose of salt.

Bank of England (BoE): The central bank and issuer of bank notes (rhyming slang for which is 'Nannies' as in nanny goats) in England and Wales. As well as acting as an ordinary bank to the Government, international organisations and other domestic and international banks, it controls the amount of money in circulation and regulates the UK banking industry. Its monetary policy committee sets the level of interest rates. It also does its best to manage the national debt in tandem with the Treasury.

Bankrupt: What we hope you won't be if you digest the contents of this book.

Bear: An investor who reckons the market is heading for a fall.

Bear Market: A market that suffers consistent falls in share prices because company profit prospects are declining. This can be caused by one or more of a number of reasons, including rising interest rates, inflation and weakening currencies. The opposite of this is a bull market.

Bid-Offer Spread: This is the difference in the buying and selling price of most investments. From the investor's point of view the cost of selling and buying any investment at any one moment in time is the spread between the two and this can vary, not only with the type of investment, but also with trading conditions and the size of the transaction.

Big Bang: The first big shake-up of the stock market in October 1986, when computers were introduced into the trading process for the first time. This was followed in 1996 by the introduction of CREST and then in 1997 by Big Bang II.

Big Bang II: October 20 1997. The use of a computer-driven trading system to cut out the middlemen in share trading, who match buyers and sellers. Initially, this was just for FTSE 100 shares, but is likely to be extended to the FTSE 250. Bid-offer spreads, rather than being reduced as was thought, actually increased especially during trading early in the day.

Blue Chip: Blue chip companies are normally household names with a consistent growth and dividend record for their shares, stable management and substantial assets. There are no strictly defined parameters for a blue chip company but they are often in the FTSE 100 Index. Examples include BP, Amoco and British Telecom.

Bond: A bond is essentially a loan. Bondholders lend money to governments or companies and are promised a certain rate of interest in return. Interest rates vary depending on the quality or reliability of the bond issuer. Government bonds, or gilts, for example, carry little risk and thus offer lower interest rates. Company bonds offer higher interest rates, with the riskiest companies' (or governments') bonds offering the highest of all and being called junk bonds.

Bourse: The French word for stock exchange — although the Frenchies have managed to get it used as a label for other stock markets too.

Broker: One who sells financial products. Be it in insurance, pensions or shares, most brokers work under compensation structures that are at direct odds with the interests of their clients. There are a lot of spivs in the business of broking since all you need is a nice patter along with a range of sharp suits.

Bull: This is the name given to the optimists who are confident that share prices will rise. The contrast is a bear who believes prices will fall. A bull stock market is one where prices are rising over the medium term and a bear market is one where they are falling.

Bull Market: A market where prices are rising and expected to continue doing so in the medium term. This is the opposite of a bear market.

CAC 40: French index of the forty biggest French companies. But most London-based brokers don't think much of it, referring to it as a load of CAC.

Call Options: Contracts that give the right — but not the obligation — to buy a fixed number of shares, for a fixed price on an agreed date in the future.

Capital: The funds of a company or an investor.

Capital Gains Tax (CGT): If you make a packet in the City those bozos at the Treasury will want their cut. This outrageous tax was introduced in 1965 as a tax on the growth, after inflation, in the value of an asset that has been sold. CGT is only charged when annual gains or profits rise above a certain level, currently a piffling £7,200 (for 2000/01), which doesn't even get you a steak sandwich in the Square Mile these days. Those selling a property that they have been living in are exempt for some reason. And no capital gains tax is payable on assets realised as a result of the death of the owner — they hit you with inheritance tax instead.

Capitalisation: The total value of a company on the stockmarket's assessment. The total market value of a company's shares is calculated by multiplying the current share price by the number of shares on issue.

Cash Flow: This represents the movement of funds through a business during a given trading period, usually a year or a quarter.

Central Bank: Normally either a government bank or the major bank in a country responsible for implementing national monetary policy and issuing government bonds. They control many aspects of a country's finances, including its money supply, regulating the banking system, underwriting and printing banknotes, lending to other banks and setting interest rates. Most are government controlled, but a few operate largely independently of the government, such as the Bundesbank in Germany.

Chief Executive: The guy in your company who takes home the most lolly. He or she is accountable to the company's board and is usually a member of that board. The chief executive (or grande fromage) is supposed to come up with all the best ideas to drive the company forward, although they usually get their lackeys to do the dirty work.

Churn: Churning is the unconscious or conscious over-trading by a stockbroker in a customer's account. Since stockbrokers are generally compensated by the number of transactions made on a customer's behalf, there is a temptation to trade for the sake of it. It's illegal, but hard to prove. We've seen it done dozens of times in the City and it's got to stop.

The City: London's financial district, which encompasses the square mile of the old City of London, bounded on the south by the Thames, on the West by the Law Courts, on the East by the Tower of London and in the North by Billingsgate Market, where something smells fishy.

Commodities: Raw materials used by industry and traded on specialist markets. There are two types of commodities. There are 'soft' commodities such as cocoa, coffee, tea, sugar and soya, and 'hard' commodities which include metals like copper, aluminium and silver. They are dealt as 'spot' commodities for immediate delivery, and 'futures' for later delivery.

Compound Interest: The investor's best friend. One hundred pounds invested in the stock market in 1918 would be worth £884,714 today. You've got to admit that that's bloody interesting.

Correction: A short, sharp shock for investors when share prices plummet — but only momentarily. Any time that stock market pundits cannot find a reason for an individual stock or the entire market falling, they call it a correction because it doesn't sound as scary as a 'crash'.

CREST: Introduced in 1996, this is a computerised system to settle up share purchases. The upside is that there are no more bits of paper passing hands any more, but the downside is that the system screws up from time to time.

Cum-Dividend: 'Cum' means 'with' in Latin. If you buy shares cum-dividend, you are buying them at a time when you will be entitled to receive the next dividend. This is as opposed to ex-dividend. If restrictions on entitlement to dividends didn't exist, people would simply buy shares the day before the dividend was due, collect it and then sell them the day after.

Dax: German index of major companies, broadly equivalent to the Dow Jones Industrial Average. Also a word traders use the morning after going out on the lash, as in: 'I got completely daxed last night.'

Day Trader: Day traders are in and out merchants who pile in and out of the market many times a day. They may not even hold a position in any securities overnight. This approach tends to generate a lot of expenses in the form of commissions and denies the day trader the ability to participate in the long-term creation of wealth through compounding that is possible if you own the shares of a quality business. It's a practice that's not for the faint-hearted and it's easy to get your fingers blow-torched off in one bad session.

Deflation: The term used when prices actually start to fall.

Depreciation: The shrinking of the pound in everyone's pocket caused by inflation is domestic depreciation. The currency of countries with high domestic inflation and balance of payments problems declines against other currencies, and this is international depreciation.

Derivatives: These are the boys that got Nick Leeson into a few problems. If shares are assets, derivatives represent contracts to buy a particular security at a given point in the future for a particular price. Options and Futures are derivatives. They can be used to lessen investment risk, but often their main attraction is that they are highly geared and can thus offer spectacular profits... and spectacular losses. The Slickers like to give them a wide berth.

Discretionary Management: A discretionary management service allows a fund manager to select a range of investments, such as unit trusts, investment trusts and shares, to put into a portfolio for a client. Discretionary services differ from managed funds or funds of funds as there is no restriction on the type of investments bought.

Discount Broker: The US term for Execution-Only Stockbroker.

Dividend: The amount paid by a company to its shareholders as their direct financial reward for holding the company's shares. Dividend per share is declared net (after tax).

Dividend Yield: The dividend over the current share price, expressed as a percentage. Different companies have different policies on the size of their dividend payouts.

Dow Jones Industrial Average: The 30 companies chosen by editors of Dow Jones & Company that are supposed to epitomise the very best American corporations and reflect the landscape of corporate America.

Eamon: City word for Old Etonians who like to waltz around the Square Mile, saying: 'Eamon Old Etonian.' The City is full of 'Eamons' and they're a smart lot although on occasion prone to acts of spivvery.

Earnings: This is the profit a company makes that is available for the shareholders of the firm. It is normally expressed as earnings per share, which is a ratio expressing the earnings over the total number of ordinary shares on the market.

Earnings Upgrade: When an analyst revises estimated earnings for a company indicating they are expecting the company to post higher profits than previously thought.

Earnings Per Share (EPS): One of the most common ways to judge a company's performance. It shows the return in money terms of what a company is generating for its investors. EPS is calculated by dividing the company's post-tax profits by the number of ordinary shares issued to date.

Enterprise Investment Scheme (EIS): The Enterprise Investment Scheme is a government incentive to help new businesses. It replaces the Business Expansion Scheme and reduces income tax liability on investments up to £100,000 a year in unquoted companies. It also avoids capital gains tax on such shares held more than five years.

Equities: The term given to investments in a company listed on a stock exchange, as opposed to fixed-interest investments and property. It is a general term for ordinary shares having an interest in the profits of a company.

Euro: The euro is the single currency introduced on January 1, 1999 for all participating countries in Europe. There are 11 countries using the euro, including Germany, France and Ireland. They all have the same interest rates. Monetary policy is decided by the European Central Bank.

Euroland: The collection of countries which joined the European single currency scheme in January. The countries are Germany, France, Italy, Spain, Belgium, Netherlands, Portugal, Austria, Ireland, Luxembourg and Finland.

European Monetary Union (EMU): The replacement of European Union member states' existing currencies with a single currency, the euro. The first phase took place on January 1, 1999 when an estimated 11 countries exchanged their currencies for the euro.

Ex-Dividend: A share sold without the right to receive the dividend payment which is marked as due to those shareholders who are on the share register at a pre-announced date. These shares have 'xd' next to their price listings in the *Financial Times*.

Execution-Only Stockbroker: Stockbrokers who offer fewer of the services championed by advisory stockbrokers, but charge cheaper transaction fees. Basically, you tell them to buy or sell a particular share and they get on and do it with no frills and no hassles. Often they hold your shares in a nominee account. Execution-only brokers are ideal for do-it-yourself investors — that's you. They are called discount brokers in the USA.

Financial Services Authority (FSA): The top investment watchdog. You can contact them on 020 7638 1240, but if you have a problem with a financial adviser or insurance company, contact the Personal Investment Authority. If you have a problem with a stockbroker, contact the Securities & Futures Authority.

Flotation: A private company is floated on the stock exchange when it issues shares for the first time. This turns it into a public limited company and it can then put the letters Plc after its name, for example Marks & Spencer Plc. Recent flotations include the travel agent Thomas Cook and the American investment bank Goldman Sachs.

FTSE 100: Also known as the Footsie, it is an index containing the 100 largest companies by market capitalisation on the London Stock Exchange. Came into being in 1984 and replaced the FT 30.

Financial Times Stock Exchange (FTSE): The key performance benchmarks for the UK stock market. The FTSE All-Share Index comprises three indices — FTSE 100, FTSE Mid 250 and FTSE Small Cap.

FTSE Small Cap: This is a stock market index that covers approximately 500 UK smaller companies between £40m and £250m in value. The index was launched in January 1993 and is calculated at the end of each business day.

Futures: Similar to options, these are contracts that give the holder the opportunity to buy a fixed number of shares, for a fixed price, on an agreed date in the future.

Gross Domestic Product (GDP): This is the total money value of all final goods and services produced in an economy in one year. In other words, the UK's GDP is the value of goods and services produced domestically by UK residents. Economists often look at GDP growth (expressed as a percentage) to see how much an economy has grown or is expected to grow during different time periods.

Gross: A figure, normally income, before the deduction of tax and/or expenses and other charges. This can be contrasted with net which means the value after the deduction of tax, costs or charges.

Growth Shares: Shares in growth companies are often bought by 'growth investors'. Growth firms have continuing growth of sales leading to earnings growth and a higher return on assets. Earnings growth is often partly attributable to extensive investment and research in product development.

Hedge Fund: Not the charity George Soros has to get bits of his garden cut back, as you might have thought. They are private funds, or limited partnerships, given greater flexibility than mutual funds to use an array of strategies such as trading short as well as long and using leverage and derivatives.

Index: An index is a valuation of something relative to time, like shares in a shares index. At the start of an index, it is given a value, normally 100, for the year it starts, allowing comparisons in the future. Indices are used by analysts to indicate general trends.

Inflation: An increase in the general level of prices in a particular economy that persists over a period of time. It reduces the purchasing power of money. Inflation is a major cause for concern for world governments, and many policies are aimed at reducing it. It is also an important concern for investors. The rise in the general level of prices can be measured through an index and the inflation rate is usually given as an annual figure for the economy. If the annual increase in prices is small and gradual, one refers to 'creeping inflation'. If inflation is way out of control like Greece's sometimes is, the term 'hyperinflation' is used.

Inland Revenue: The boys who do their best to screw your profits out of you if you make some cash. If you're at all interested you can pay them a visit at: http://www.open.gov.uk/inrev/irhome.htm — it's a gas.

Insider Dealing: Also known as insider trading, this is when individuals buy or sell shares based on information only made available to them and not the whole marketplace. It is an illegal activity in most countries although very difficult to prove, thank God.

Initial Public Offering (IPO): The US name for a company's first sale of shares to the public. In the UK we call it a New Issue.

Institutions: Institutional investors include pension funds and unit trusts. These are the big players in the stock market as they have a lot of money to invest, and as major shareholders they often have a say in company decisions. Anyone remember the Ice Maiden, Carol Galley? She's the gal at Mercury Asset Management who cast her vote in favour of Granada in its takeover of Forte. Thanks a bunch, doll!

Investment Trust: A closed-end investment fund which is listed as a company on the Stock Exchange. It invests in other shares, usually in a specific sector or world region. Boring but safe, most of the time.

Junk Bond: Bonds that fall below 'investment grade'. This means Standard & Poor's and Moody's credit rating agencies have given them a rating below treble-B. This means they have a high level of risk. They have been widely issued in the US for a number of years as a method for companies to borrow money, and although the European and UK junk bond markets are relatively immature, they are expected to expand rapidly in the next few years.

Large Cap: Companies with a large market capitalisation — the number of ordinary shares in issue multiplied by the current share price. Financial organisations judge companies' sizes differently but according to the Companies Act 1985 (amended 1989) a large cap usually has two of the following: more than 250 employees, assets of over £4m or turnover in excess of £8m.

Liquidity: An expression commonly used by fund managers to indicate how frequently a share or security is traded. The greater the liquidity, the more frequently traded a share is and the easier it is for an investor to deal. When a fund manager talks about liquidity within a portfolio it usually refers to the amount of cash within the fund.

Listed Company: A Public Limited Company (plc), listed on a stock exchange.

Lloyd's: One of the largest insurance markets, Lloyd's insures against almost any risk there is. The corporation has members, who are brokers or underwriters, who must deposit substantial sums of collateral, and 'names', who deposit capital and pledge their assets to Lloyd's, receiving income without having any executive responsibility.

M&A: An abbreviation for mergers and acquisitions. If you ever meet anyone at a party who says they work in M&A it generally pays to give them a wide berth — unless they can give you some inside information, of course.

Managed Funds: Funds which contain three asset classes — equities, bonds and cash, with a minimum proportion of 50% in sterling. 35% must be in UK equities, 10% in foreign equities, another 10% must be held in UK bonds or gilts, non-UK Government or corporate bonds, cash or property.

Margin: Borrowing money to use specifically for buying securities of any kind in a brokerage account. Or, a measure of profitability of a company, like profit margin, operating margin or gross margin.

Market Capitalisation: The number of shares issued multiplied by the share price at the time of market capitalisation calculation.

Market Makers: Those who create a market in a particular stock (a share or a bond for instance) by continually quoting prices at which they will buy or sell on demand. The existence of market makers means that a private investor will almost always be able to sell a holding.

Mid Cap: Companies with a medium-sized market capitalisation — the number of ordinary shares in issue multiplied by the current share price. According to the Companies Act 1985 (amended 1989) a mid cap usually has two of the following; up to 250 employees, assets of up to £4m or turnover of up to £8m. However, '85 was a long time ago now.

Mutual Organisation: A mutual organisation is an organisation such as a building society or friendly society jointly owned by its members who get all the benefits and profits from the activities. 'Carpetbaggers' open accounts in the major societies in the hope of a windfall if demutualisation proceeds.

Nasdaq: A national US stock market where trades are made exclusively via computers. The second largest market in the country, the Nasdaq is home to many high-tech and newer firms, including Microsoft. It now has its own website for UK investors: http://www.nasdaq.co.uk.

Net Asset Value (NAV): In the case of investment trusts, which are companies in structure, this is value of the underlying shares of the trust minus its liabilities.

Net: A figure, usually income, after charges, such as tax, have been deducted.

Net Income Reinvested: Any dividends generated by the fund are automatically reinvested net at the basic rate of tax to show the total return.

New Issue: The first time a company is floated on the stock market. Selling your company, or a part of it, to outside investors is a way to raise money for expansion plans.

New York Stock Exchange (NYSE): The largest and oldest stock exchange in the United States, this Wall Street haunt is the one frequently featured on television, with hundreds of traders on the floor staring up at screens and answering phones, ready to trade stocks upon command from their firms.

Nominee Account: A type of account in which execution-only stockbrokers tend to hold shares belonging to clients, to make buying and selling of those shares easier. It does mean, however, that any shareholder perks are unlikely to be enjoyed by the investor.

Offshore Investments: Offshore investments are not necessarily only for the super-rich or for those wishing to hide money in Swiss bank accounts. They are simply any savings and investments which are placed in a region outside UK tax law.

Option: Generic term for financial contracts that bestow the right — but not the commitment — to buy or sell a fixed number of shares at a fixed price at an agreed date in the future.

Ordinary Shares: These are also known as equities, and in the US are called common stock. The shareholder is protected so their maximum loss is the value of their shares and they are not liable for the full debts of a company. Most ordinary shares have voting rights.

Outperform: When an investment instrument, such as a share or index, performs better than a given benchmark. The Slicker portfolio outperformed the Footsie by over 100% last year.

Overweight: When there is a significant holding (or weighting) in a particular investment or sector relative to other funds in the same investment category or an established index.

Penny Share: A share of very low market capitalisation (often a few million pounds) trading in multiples of just a few pence. They are very volatile and subject to extreme price fluctuations on the flimsiest of rumours, which is why we love 'em.

Portfolio Management: Give all your cash to a stockbroker and say: 'Here you are, mate — go and manage my wedge.'

Preference Shares: Preference shares are part of share capital of the issuing company. If the company goes into liquidation, preference share holders rank after creditors, but before ordinary shareholders.

Premium: Also usually applied to an investment trust. Where the share price of the trust is greater than the value of the underlying shares the trust is holding it is said to be at a premium because investors are paying over the odds for the right to invest in the underlying shares.

Price/Book Ratio (P/B): This is the company's share price divided by its net asset value. This is an estimation of the value of the company based on its assets. These will be everything from property, cash deposits, investments and products it has not yet sold. It is used by fund managers and professional investors when deciding whether to buy shares in a company.

Price/earnings Ratio (P/E): This is also used in investment analysis and is the company's share price divided by its earnings per share. Earnings per share is calculated by dividing the net profit by the number of ordinary shares the company has issued. The lower the P/E ratio the 'better value' the holding. The higher the P/E, the greater is the expectation in terms of increased future profitability. The price-earnings ratio is sometimes called the 'multiple' of the company.

ProShare: A pressure group representing the interests of the private investor. They publish a magazine called, *The Investor*, and also have a useful information pack on how to set up a share club. Our advice is to contact them on 020 7220 1730 and get on the mailing list for all their freebie information.

Public Limited Company (plc): As opposed to private, a

company is public after it issues partial ownership of itself, in the form of shares, to the public. Only plcs can be listed on the London Stock Exchange or the Alternative Investment Market.

Put Option: Contracts that give the right — but not the obligation — to sell a fixed number of shares, for a fixed price on an agreed date in the future.

Retail Price Index: The RPI is a method of measuring inflation and is calculated from the price of a basket of family goods. The weightings of each item are adjusted occasionally to reflect the changing average in shopping habits, but food accounts for 6%, while housing accounts for 20%, motoring 14% and alcohol 7% of the index. The index shows that the same amount of goods, which would have cost £1 to buy in 1900, would have risen to £66.50 by 1998.

Revenue: The money a company collects from a customer for a product or service.

Rights Issue: A rights issue takes place when a company wishes to raise more capital via an additional issue of shares. The company gives current shareholders preferential treatment by allowing them to buy the new shares in proportion to their current holdings before the shares come to market. The purpose is to ensure current shareholder's holdings are not diluted by the issue of new shares. The rights issue offer is made by way of a letter which is valid for 21 days. The shareholder can sell the letter, use it to buy their allotted shares, or let it lapse. If the last option is taken, the company's underwriting stockbroker will sell the unwanted shares and send the cash proceeds to the shareholders.

Sausage & Mash: A piece of rhyming slang for 'cash' that is widely used by the Slickers when they do well on a deal.

Scrip Issue (also known as a Bonus Issue): A scrip issue is similar to a rights issue, but the shares have zero value — in effect, they are 'free' shares. During a scrip issue, shareholders are awarded bonus shares in proportion to their current holdings. Typically, a 1 for 3 scrip issue means that for every three shares you currently hold, you get a new one free. But if you hold US shares a 1 for 3 scrip issue is confusingly called a '4 for 3 split' — before you had three shares, now you have 4.

Securities: Generic term for shares and bonds and options.

Securities & Futures Authority (SFA): The people who regulate your stockbroker and spread betting firm. Phone number: 020 7378 9000.

SETS: SETS stands for Stock Exchange Electronic Trading System. It is used to buy and sell shares in the FTSE 100. Companies that are on the waiting list to enter the FTSE 100 are also traded on SETS, as are companies that fall out of the FTSE 100 if they become too small. SETS is an order-driven system which means that orders to buy and sell shares are automatically matched by the SETS computer to give the best possible price. Smaller companies are traded on SEAQ and those with only one broker or less are traded on SEATS PLUS.

Share: A security which represent part ownership of a company.

Share Capital: The share capital of a company is that part of a company which is divided into shares and owned by the shareholders. Share capital is also called equity. It is distinct from a company's debt, which can include corporate bonds which are issued and traded on the stock exchange. Equity and debt together make up the total capital 'employed' in a company.

Share Club: Group of investors which meets regularly to discuss which shares to buy and sell out of a common fund.

Shareholder: If you buy even one share in a company, you can proudly call yourself a shareholder. As a shareholder you get an invitation to the company's annual meeting, and you have the right to vote on the members of the Board of Directors and other company matters.

Share Premium: When a company floats it can generally sell its shares for a substantially higher price than their face value. This difference between the nominal value and the sale price is the share premium which companies show in their balance sheets under the share premium account.

Share Split: When the share price of a company becomes too large the firm often issues additional shares, reducing the overall value of all its shares on the market. This works because shares are like a slice of cake. The more slices issued the smaller each slice will become. Shares are often split for cosmetic reasons. Lower priced shares can be easier to market as people feel they are getting more shares for the same amount of money.

Small Cap: Companies with a small market capitalisation — the number of ordinary shares in issue multiplied by the current share price. According to the Companies Act 1985 (amended 1989) a small cap usually has two of the following: up to 50 employees, assets of up to £975,000 or turnover of up to £2m. Basically, our favourite companies and the ones where there is some quick sausage & mash (qv) to be made.

Spivs: What the old Current Bun (The *Sun*) branded us when it was revealed that we liked to have a punt in the market. It is generally a term applied to City folk who favour a very wide pinstripe.

Stamp Duty: A rubbishy little tax payable on purchase of ordinary shares, as well as preference shares and convertible loan stocks. All governments want to encourage wider share ownership and would be able to do it if they didn't tax stock market punters into oblivion. When will they learn?

Stochastics: We've never bothered with these but the experts tell us they measure the position of a stock, market, or industry group average as compared with its most recent trading range, indicating oversold and overbought conditions. But whenever anyone mentions stochastics to us our eyes glaze over and a fair amount of yawning goes on.

Stock: Exactly the same as a share and used more commonly in the States. Investors purchase stock as a way to own a part of a publicly quoted business.

Stockbroker: A middleman, often a spiv, who buys and sells shares on your behalf and earns a whopping commission on the transaction. For professional integrity they're in the same league as prostitutes, pimps, accountants and journalists like us.

Stock Exchange: A place where stocks and shares are bought and sold. The London Stock Exchange is the granddaddy of them all in Europe and is much bigger and better than anything they've got in Germany — one reason why the Jerries want a merger.

Ticker Symbol: An abbreviation for a company's name which is used as shorthand by share quote reporting services and various online sites. We had some fun with a company called Corporate Executive Search whose ticker symbol was CEX. We used to ring up all our mates in the City and ask them how much they paid for CEX, which is about as funny as things ever get in the Sqaure Mile.

Top-Down: A type of investment strategy where fund managers or investors are governed by economic considerations and take a wider perspective by investing in specific themes such as industrial sectors, countries or geographic regions.

Tracker Funds: These funds aim to mirror the performance of a given stock market index, usually the FTSE All-Share or FTSE 100. The fund manager spreads his investment in exact proportion to the weighting, or proportional value, of companies in the index.

Treasury: Mr Blair's accounts department. If you're perverse enough to want to find out more you can visit them at: http://www.hm-treasury.gov.uk/

Trouser: A verb that is used a lot by the Slickers to describe someone who has done better than expected out of a deal, e.g. Luke Johnson trousered £50 million personally by selling X to Y. It is often used when we want to meet someone. We used it about Nomura's top boy, Guy Hands, and he invited us around to Nomura House for lunch and a good chat.

Underperform: When an investment instrument, such as a share or index, performs worse than a given benchmark. You can often pick up some great recovery prospects by choosing companies that are fundamentally good businesses but which have underperformed the market by 30% or more.

Underweight: When a portfolio or fund has significantly less investment in a specific sector than either the benchmark or others in the same peer group.

Underwriter/Underwritten: The stockbrokers — we prefer to call them undertakers — who help a company come public in a New Issue. They underwrite (vouch for) the stock. When a company has been brought public, the shares have been underwritten.

Valuation: The determination of a fair value for a security. It's very difficult to say what a company is worth and sometimes the analysts screw it up — but their valuations are better than nowt.

Venture Capital Trust (VCT): A cunning investment wheeze allowing individuals to put up to £100,000 a year into small, unquoted companies. Investors are exempt from income tax on dividends from VCT shares, while subscribers to new shares are entitled to claim 20% relief if they are held for five years.

Venture Capital: Venture capital is money offered by individuals or institutions for investments in new or developing businesses where the capital is provided usually in exchange for shares (equity) in the business. Remember that guy who gave Anita Roddick £10,000 to set up the Body Shop? He trousered £100 million when the company went public — lucky chap!